The Hidden Children of the Goddess

Embrace Wicca, Become Strong, Be at Peace with Yourself and the World Around You

Moonwater SilverClaw

Founder of TheHiddenChildrenoftheGoddess.com,
the blog with readers in over 173 countries

from GoddessHasYourBack.com

A QuickBreakthrough Publishing Edition

More copies are available from the publisher with the imprint QuickBreakthrough Publishing. For more information about this book contact: askawitchnow@gmail.com   This book was developed and written with care. Names and details were modified to respect privacy.

Other Books by Moonwater SilverClaw:

- Goddess Has Your Back
- Goddess Walks Beside You
- Goddess Reveals Your Enchanted Light
- Beyond the Law of Attraction to Real Magick

Praise for *The Hidden Children of the Goddess:*

"Moonwater brings Wicca to life, enveloping you in the mystery and magick of the Craft. Her writing talent is amazing! Her kindness and even sense of fun is ever present throughout her writing. Moonwater expresses profound Wicca concepts through examples in her own life experience. Wicca actually saved her life and empowered her to leave an abusive marriage, and this shows the power of this sacred path to positively change the course of our lives, too. Moonwater's stories personally inspire me, and I am confident that they will inspire you also." – Rev. Patrick McCollum, internationally recognized spiritual leader, the 2010 recipient of the Mahatma Gandhi Award for the Advancement of Religious Pluralism.

"Moonwater's writing [includes] a portrait of a woman who lives her faith, and whose life was saved by it. Because so many lives, my own included, were irrevocably changed by Wicca, were given new focus, new purpose, and perhaps most importantly, new personal power to realize one's dreams and ambitions . . . [this is] a story about making your own happy endings, about rescuing yourself." – Jason Pitzl-Waters, blogger at WildHunt.org

"*The Hidden Children of the Goddess* is a well-written, fresh look into the basics of Wicca. Moonwater infused the book with stories from her own spiritual journey. At times it almost feels as if a close friend or trusted mentor were explaining the ins and outs of the Wiccan experience. Rather than saying, 'Here's how it's done,' the book extends its hand and says, 'Here, let me show you.' Many books are published on the basics of Wicca. This book stands out due to the warmth of Moonwater's writing style and her very personal approach. I would certainly recommend this book to a seeker, one of my students, or even those of other religions who are curious about Wiccan practice." – Heather Greene, writer, Wiccan Priestess, columnist, blogger, www.miraselena.com

"This is like sharing a nice cup of coffee with a new friend, while you two are taking a walk in the woods. Moonwater has a LOT to teach all of us, from the young person who wants to know why she feels 'special, ' to us seasoned practitioners of Wicca." – Angus McMahan, blogger, http://www.patheos.com/blogs/askangus/

Visit Moonwater SilverClaw's blog:
GoddessHasYourBack.com

Foreword

When I first met Moonwater I realized what a remarkable, compassionate person she is. Over time, I've seen how she works hard to kindly serve and encourage others through her spirituality and found myself moved by her dedication.

In this book, Moonwater showcases exactly how Wicca has influenced her, and how it can also benefit your personal journey. She brings Wicca to life, enveloping you in the mystery and magick of the Craft. Her writing talent is amazing!

In my work towards world peace and sustainability, I have opportunities to meet extraordinary individuals. In Thailand, I was an honored guest at a gathering of over 150,000 Buddhist monks from around the world at the Dhammakaya Temple in the Pathumtani Province. The gathered Buddhists gave me the title World Inner Peace Ambassador. I mention this because I know personally there is a compassionate energy that truly spiritual people radiate. And Moonwater has such a benevolent energy.

Her kindness and even sense of fun are ever present throughout her book, *The Hidden Children of the Goddess*, and its message comes through loud and clear to the reader.

Moonwater expresses profound Wicca concepts through examples in her own life experience. Wicca actually saved her life and empowered her to leave an abusive marriage, and this shows the power of this sacred path to positively change the course of our lives, too. Moonwater's stories personally inspire me, and I am confident that they will inspire you also.

Through the well-written and wisdom-filled pages of *The Hidden Children of the Goddess*, you'll not only learn to expand your life and incorporate Wicca into your day to day living, but to also create a framework that brings you closer to the sacred.

The Gods Moonwater presents are real and her book serves as a powerful guide toward developing a deep personal relationship with them in your own life.

I recommend this book highly to all who would read it.

- Rev. Patrick McCollum

Reverend Patrick McCollum is an internationally recognized spiritual leader in the Pagan/Earth-Based religions whose work toward human rights, social justice, and equality for all religions and spiritual traditions, transcends cultural, religious, and political barriers. Reverend McCollum is the 2010 recipient of the Mahatma Gandhi Award for the Advancement of Religious Pluralism. Reverend McCollum's spiritual work focuses on seeing the sacred within each and every human being and bringing together people of all spiritual paths, to work together toward global sustainability and world peace. Through religion and spirituality Reverend McCollum brings a new message of planetary consciousness on a global level that will alert the world to the sacredness of our connection with Divinity and with each other. You can read more about Reverend McCollum and his organization at www.patrickmccollum.org

Introduction

Wicca is a chronically misunderstood faith, sometimes even by those who've had first-hand experiences with it. Perhaps this is why we need to be reacquainted with it over and over again, the basics gone over, the handshakes and smiles delivered on cue. For the longtime veterans of the Pagan scene Moonwater's book will mostly likely not shock or deliver you some unknown aspect of the Craft, but it will give you a portrait of a woman who lives her faith, and whose life was saved by it. I think this is something we "undersell" in our ranks, the salvic power of becoming, or realizing, one's essential Witch self, of their connection to nature, the gods, and the universe. Because so many lives, my own included, were irrevocably changed by Wicca, were given new focus, new purpose, and perhaps most importantly, new personal power to realize one's dreams and ambitions.

This is a book of basics, but it is also a book about new beginnings, about how our common bonds as siblings within the Craft are quietly causing a revolution in the way we think, act, and behave. It's a story about making your own happy endings, about rescuing yourself, and that, I believe, is what makes books like this necessary. This is why you are holding a "Wicca 101" book in your hands, because for someone out there (maybe you) this is that first essential step. Someone's life is being saved as you read this, and I will never begrudge a new book on Wicca for that precise reason.

- Jason Pitzl-Waters, The Wild Hunt http://wildhunt.org/

Jason Pitzl-Walter's Biography:

Since launching "The Wild Hunt" in 2004, Jason Pitzl-Waters has become one of the leading voices for analysis and insight into how modern Pagan faiths are represented within the mainstream media. In addition, "The Wild Hunt" has also conducted in-depth interviews with prominent figures within modern Paganism, academia, and religion journalism. Jason wants to raise the level of discourse and journalism on important issues within the modern Pagan and Heathen communities, while advocating a broader commitment to encouraging religious multiplicity and solidarity (where appropriate) with surviving indigenous and non-monotheistic faith groups.

In addition to his work with The Wild Hunt, Jason has also written for *newWitch Magazine, PanGaia Magazine, Thorn Magazine*, and *Llewellyn Worldwide*. He also maintains a weekly podcast entitled "A Darker Shade of Pagan" that explores underground music from a Pagan perspective.

Jason is a former Board of Director member of Cherry Hill Seminary, and is coordinating The Pagan Newswire Collective, an open collective of Pagan journalists, newsmakers, media liaisons, and writers who are interested in sharing and promoting primary-source reporting from within our interconnected communities.

You can contact Jason at jpitzl@gmail.com

CONTENTS

DEDICATION AND ACKNOWLEDGEMENTS

This book is dedicated to the God and Goddess. Thanks to Sherry Lusk, Kay Pannell, Stacy D. Horn, and Tom Marcoux for editing. Thanks to Judita Bacinskaite for rendering this book's front cover. Thanks to Patrick McCollum, Jason Pitzl-Waters, Angus McMahan and Heather Greene for your kind support. Thanks to people who attend my workshops. Thanks to the readers from over 173 countries of my blog: GoddessHasYourBack.com

CHAPTER 1:
WHAT IS WICCA?

You may be reading this book because you somehow felt out of place or even stifled by a religion you encountered. Maybe you're simply curious. Perhaps you've had some unexplained experiences. I know I have. I've seen amazing things, and I'll share how Wicca actually saved my life.

Have you ever felt different during the full moon? Ever wonder where Deity is and if you could connect with Deity? By the way, I will use the word *Deity* to represent all the Gods and Goddesses together. Some people might think of Deity as Higher Power.

Let's continue. Do you have questions like: "Who practices Wicca?" and "What is Wicca?"

When I say the word *witch*, do you think of an old green-skinned woman who eats children and cackles while flying on her broom? Or are these just bedtime stories to scare children? Who are witches really?

Witches are everyday people. No, we aren't green and warty. From soccer moms to construction workers, we look just like any other person. We eat breakfast, go to work or school, and have friends and family. The only difference is our faith.

In short, Wiccans are *The Hidden Children of the Goddess*. In this book, I draw back the curtain and the shadows and reveal what the Hidden Children are all about. (Okay, so this book spoils the "hidden" part. I guess I should have called it "The Revealed Children of the Goddess.")

By the way, you will notice as you go along that I use the words *Wicca* and *Witchcraft* interchangeably. There is some debate about these terms and how they may be used. But for the purposes of this book, they will mean the same thing.

As for why I took on this project, I feel that I was invited, if not compelled, by the Gods and Goddesses to write this book. Why? When I first started with Wicca, most of the books available were like textbooks. Not only were they dull, but they were also difficult to read, especially for a dyslexic like me. My goal with this book is to give you both a pleasant and an easy reading experience.

The book in your hands covers a wide variety of useful information to help the neophyte understand the Hidden Children, and it provides a basic understanding of Wicca and how you, if you so choose, can practice it. Beginning students of Wicca will find this book helpful as a general reference. I'll also share with you some of the practices we use.

For instance, did you know Wiccans can raise a temple anywhere? While Christians go to a brick and mortar church, Wiccans can use anything from the natural outdoors to someone's living room to practice our faith. We don't have to be in a specific place to worship the Gods. Although we prefer natural settings, any place can be sacred space. I once held a circle in my bathroom! Granted, it was a little cramped, but it was the only space available at the time in my small home. But hey, it worked! In fact, the experience was very interesting.

Numerous Buddhists devote much time in meditation. Wiccans often meditate, but we also meet in joyous gatherings and invite the Gods to participate. And They do!

Yes, Wiccans have many Gods while Christians have one. Wiccans find each God has a different expertise that affects our lives. We can go to these different Gods and know that there is a specialist for each problem or challenge we face. We want the right expert for the right advice and help we need. Would you ask your grandma to shingle your roof? No! You'd want an expert roofer to handle the job. Similarly, you wouldn't go to Mars, the God of war, to find a peaceful resolution to a conflict. Instead, you might seek Eirene for guidance.

Besides having many Gods, Wiccans focus on the rhythms of the Earth and how nature dances to those rhythms. We appreciate the Earth's cycles, the turning of the seasons, and the waxing and waning of the moon. Attuning ourselves to these cycles creates a wholeness and balance in our lives and helps us be closer to our Gods.

The more you know about Wicca, the more you can harmonize yourself to the cycles of the natural world. This book will help you understand the ways of the Hidden Children of the Goddess and help you synchronize yourself to the cycles of nature.

Wiccans understand these rhythms as corresponding with different stages of life and the cycles contained within life. We believe in the old Gods, among them Isis, Odin, Freyja, Cernnunos, and Pan. These Gods and Goddesses are archetypes of the Lord and Lady (the God and Goddess) and represent all of nature.

Before you started this book, you may have heard that Wiccans are witches. This is true, but you need to realize that not all witches are Wiccan—although all Wiccans are witches. Confused? Okay, let's look at it in a different way: all Lutherans are Christian, but not all Christians are Lutherans. I hope that helps.

Just like Christianity, Wicca has many kinds of Wicca, or as we call them, Traditions—such as Gardnerian, Alexandrian, and Dianic. This book will introduce one that is a bit more eclectic (that is, from many different traditions).

A Word on Traditions

What is a "Tradition" in Wicca? It's commonly called a "Trad," and it's a system of rituals and beliefs that a particular group follows. One Trad is Dianic which is known for its worship of a single Goddess and having a focus on feminism.

Another Trad is Gardnerian Wicca. Gerald B. Gardner, considered by many as "the Father of Wicca," stated that the New Forest Coven initiated him into their group in 1939. Many consider Gardnerian Wicca to be the earliest Wiccan Trad–from which many other Trads sprouted.

Trads come in many forms. Just like Christianity has many forms, the Trads in Wicca form different groups with different ways of doing things.

I find that the essence of a Trad is that it gets a person closer to Deity.

Unfortunately, much Wiccan knowledge has been fragmented sometimes due to people splitting off before they learned more and deeper knowledge.

At this point, I invite us of the Wiccan spirituality to realize that we all hold pieces of the same picture. However, none of us can see this picture by ourselves because we only hold a few of the original pieces.

We need to all gather together to make a whole picture. Coming together, we will be better able to see our own "missing pieces" and collect these missing pieces of knowledge. Then we can restore our own pieces to the larger puzzle.

If we don't do this, much of what was learned and known will be forgotten. This piecing back together of the puzzle is something we all need to do. If we don't, we may lose something very dear.

So let's keep our community strong! Let's get to know each other and respect our differences because there's something to learn from someone different.

Wiccan Traditions and the Degree System

A number of Wiccan traditions have a degree system. A degree is defined as a stage of knowledge that has been learned. You might call it a "level."

Many Trads have three levels or degrees. Some have more; others have less. Most British Trads have three.

My own Trad includes:

1) First Degree

When someone first approaches the Wicca path, they are called a seeker. After learning basic material, a newly initiated person may earn the level of *first degree*. The person, now known as a First Degree learns certain basic rituals including calling quarters and casting a circle.

2) Second Degree

After learning deeper and secret practices, one may rise to second degree. To rise to this second level is called *elevation*.

The Second Degree will know enough to do some teaching of seekers and first degrees. A Third Degree supervises a Second Degree's teaching sessions. The Second degree may have other responsibilities, too. This varies based on one's Trad and from coven to coven.

3) Third Degree

To qualify for elevation to third degree, a Second Degree must demonstrate a number of more complex and secret skills in rituals and even leadership skills. Why? A Third Degree can start a new coven (called "hiving off").

The standards for degrees can very widely from group to group. Again, the above examples are more representative of British Trads in Wicca.

The Wiccan Rede

Now back to Christians. Christians follow a code of morals called the Ten Commandments. We follow a code of morals, too. It is called *The Wiccan Rede*, and it states:

Eight words the Wiccan Rede fulfill, An it harm none, do what ye will.
— *Doreen Valiente (1922-1999)*

The first published form of this couplet comes from a speech by Doreen Valiente in 1964. Note that the Wiccan Rede (meaning advice or council) is a statement that provides the key moral system of the Wiccan faith. Yes, I know it is impossible to harm none. (Many of us eat bacon. Even carrots have to be cut down. I know plenty of carrot-killers.) The Wiccan Rede *guides* us to do no harm when at all possible. Sowing, harvesting, and eating are part of the cycle of life. Life feeds life. But to cause unnecessary harm is wrong and should never be done. Now let's look at why.

The Law of Three

Now just when you thought you were free and clear to do anything you wanted, let's talk about the Law of Three, also known as the "Threefold Law of Return." Not to say you can't do anything you want, but there are consequences to your actions.

Here is how it works: Whatever energy you send out into the universe will get magnified threefold and returned to you. It is a simple principle, but when seen in action it can become quite complex.

Imagine standing in front of a pond, a Universal Pond, representing the universe. You have some stones in your pocket. These stones represent the actions you take in life and the energy you send out into the universe when you take those actions. You drop a stone into the Pond; this creates a ripple of energy upon the Universal Pond.

The ripples (the energies of the action you sent out) *grow in magnitude*. Eventually they hit the edge of the Pond in their amplified state and bounce back to you in their stronger form. This could be good, or it could be bad depending on what action you originally took.

Just like nature on Earth, the universe has a self-regulating system that many people call Karma. Karma is a system of belief in which any action done in life has an effect that will balance out that action either in this life or in the next reincarnation.

Getting back to the Pond, imagine that you stand before the Universal Pond with your friend John. John takes out his own stone and drops it in (symbolizing his own actions in the universe). You drop your own stone into the Pond. Both of you watch the ripples, but then something new happens: The ripples collide with each other, creating a third type of ripple (or energy in the universe).

Now, not only does your energy come back to you from the edge of the pond, but John's energy ripple comes back and hits you, too. And then that third energy ripple hits you both when it comes back as well. These energies can merge together and create a stronger effect, too.

With all the people on this planet, it can be very complex because there are many ripples in the universe. Everyone you know and even people you don't are making ripples that can affect you. For example, a politician can affect you with the policies she makes, and you probably don't personally know her. With all the ripples occurring every day, it's hard to see how one action will affect you. Let's look at the following example.

You've made plans to meet up with Kate, Sam's sister. Unfortunately, Sam forgot to pick her up from work that day. Now you're disappointed that you couldn't see your friend Kate, and you are mad at Sam for his forgetfulness. Sam's behavior affects you and Kate.

In this case, the third ripple of energy is Kate, who is also mad at Sam for not picking her up. This energy can collide with you, too. Kate's irritation with Sam can cause her to be grumpy. And that can lead to Kate starting an argument with you!

People are dropping stones into the Pond every day and all day—not to mention those people who like to skip their stones across the pond. There are always some of those folks.

Now there are ripples everywhere, bouncing off each other and everyone. Now, imagine that some of these ripples are formed by good and kind acts. Those acts will be magnified threefold and returned to the kind people. This is when the Law can be a blessing.

However, bad or baneful acts will also be returned threefold! This is why Wiccans try to only practice positive loving acts and gestures. We stay away from doing bad actions for the above obvious reasons.

Here is a real life example of the Law of Three in action. As a teacher who struggled to make ends meet, my friend Sarah just wasn't getting enough work even though people really liked her classes. But she still gave free workshops to help people out of work find jobs. She taught résumé skills and job interview techniques to those who needed to learn them.

One of her workshop attendees, Mark, found Sarah to be a good teacher, and he decided to introduce her to a director at a local college. Soon Sarah was teaching multiple classes at that college. Giving her time freely was a positive act, and it came back to Sarah more than threefold! And Mark gained favor with the college director because he gave her a good referral.

I've enjoyed positive results with the Threefold Law. For example, one day I went to the gym. A woman saw my knitting project bursting from my shoulder bag and invited me to join a group of older women who do crafts. (I knit, among other things.) After a while, the group learned of my proficiency with computers.

One day, Janis, one of the craft women, mentioned her problems with her computer. So I offered to go over to her home and take a look. After I solved her computer problems, Janis caught my arm at the door. She insisted on giving me some money. I never asked for money; I was doing it as a friend. Still, she insisted.

Now you may say: "That's nice. But how does this apply to the Law of Three?" Offering my time to help another with no intention of receiving payment helped me. This action helped spread word of my talents. Now I have a number of clients who pay me to fix their computers.

Origin of the Words Wicca or Witch

Now let's look at the origin of the words Wicca or Witch. It wasn't always a bad name or derogatory insult to someone. To help us understand where these words come from, let's look at a quote from the book *A History of Witchcraft: Sorcerers, Heretics & Pagans, Second Edition,* by Jeffrey B. Russell and Brooks Alexander (Thames & Hudson, 2007).

> The ultimate origin the English word 'witch' is the Indo-European root *weik, which has to do with religion and magic. *Weik produced four families of derivatives:
>
> 1. *wih-l, which yielded Old English wiggle, 'sorcery', and wiglera, 'sorcerer', and through Old and Middle French, modern English 'guile'. Also Old English wil, Middle and modern English 'wile', 2. Old Norse *wihl-, 'Craftiness'.
> 3. *wik-, 'holy' whence Old High German wihen and German weihen, 'to consecrate'; Middle German wick, 'holy', and Latin victima, 'sacrifice'. 4. *wick-, 'magic, sorcery', whence Middle German wikken, 'to predict', and Old English wicca, wicce, 'witch', and wiccian, 'to work sorcery,

bewitch'. From wicca derives Middle English witche and modern 'witch'.

Different from *wiek and its derivations is *weik, 'bending', whence Old English wiccan, 'to bend', from which the modern English 'weak' and 'witchelm'. Related to wiccan are Old Saxon wikan, Old High German wichan, Old Norse vikja, all meaning 'to bend, or turn aside'.

Old English witan, 'to know' and all related words including 'sise' are totally unrelated to either of the above.

Witches, therefore, were the ones who "predicted" or "worked sorcery" to help see and change the world around them. If our ancestors were experiencing a drought, the witch was able to see if rain was coming. This insight helped the people make necessary preparations, making sure that the people had food to eat and wouldn't starve.

But now that we know where the names come, we can look at some other aspects of Wicca.

Covens

A coven is a group of witches. This is one option for witches who like to practice with others. Many people think a coven has to have thirteen members in order to be called such. Not true.

A coven can consist of only three members. Or the High Priestess and High Priest may have as large a group as they can handle. This can be determined simply by how many the meeting place can accommodate.

Covens are like an extended family with each person

bringing something that only they can bring to the group. Therefore, each coven is unique and has very close relationships among its members.

Covens have a rule: "What is said in circle stays in circle." Sort of like Vegas, but in this case it's true. What is the reason for this? Being in circle is being in sacred space. So anything done or said in this sacred space isn't for the outside world to know. Because of this rule, much isn't known to those outside Wicca. Such secrecy causes many of the misunderstandings about what Wicca is. This is another reason why we are known as the Hidden Children. Wicca is considered a mystery tradition, something veiled in shadow, whose knowledge is available only for the initiated.

In a coven, trust is very important. It gives rise to our saying, "In perfect love and perfect trust to the Goddess." You most often hear it phrased "in perfect love and perfect trust." The trust part is in the Gods, that they will guide us to where we need to be.

We also trust in our coven mates. We need both trust in our Gods and in our coven mates to have a successful and productive coven. We need to be comfortable within our circle in order to work good magick. Many times we are working on very personal issues with the Gods and each other to help us grow and become more. Who wants to talk about one's health problem if Jim is going to blab about it later to someone outside the circle?

So trust needs to be present.

And why do spell magick with a "k" at the end? Yes, I'm dyslexic, but no, that isn't the reason. The simple answer is this: Adding the "k" at the end of the word differentiates the sleight-of-hand magic you see performed on stage from the real magick that we use in our Craft.

My Personal Awakening

I grew up in a traditional church that taught the traditional lessons about "God." As a little girl, I always wondered why religious people said one thing but did the opposite. They would say, "Love one another," yet they didn't. They said, "Treat everyone with love," but they didn't. I didn't understand how we could all be God's children when it seemed He loved only some of his children and not others. I was told He hated gays and lesbians and would punish anyone who didn't do exactly as He said. *The Bible* tells stories of how God would punish those who didn't obey his strict rules by sending them to a terrible place to suffer and burn forever! How could He do that to his children? I thought He loved all his children.

It was these contradictions along with so many others that made me turn from the church and from "God." I didn't want anything to do with a God that was so cruel. I stopped going to church.

As a little girl, I loved the outdoors and preferred playing with animals to going to church. I was happier in the forests and in the wild places of nature than sitting on a pew. I remember noticing that I never saw a cat hating another cat because of its color, size, or shape. Cats do not dislike other cats because of their appearance. Cats naturally respond to others according to how they are treated. I decided that I preferred this path of nature.

One day I heard a word, "Wicca." I didn't know what it was or what it meant, but it sounded interesting, so I wanted to know more. I went to my local bookshop and asked the lady at the counter. She enthusiastically led me to the section on Wicca, and I was awestruck by all the books I saw there. The woman helping me was Wiccan. As she began stacking books upon books in my arms, I asked her which one book would be best to start with. She handed me *Wicca: A Guide for the Solitary Practitioner* by Scott Cunningham (Llewellyn Publications, 1989).

I started reading it that night, and everything clicked. Scott Cunningham wrote: "Unlike some religions, Wicca doesn't view Deity as distant. The Goddess and God are both within ourselves and manifest in all nature. This is the universality; there is nothing that isn't of the Gods." I understood immediately; the Gods were part of everything. I had always known this. I could always feel them whenever I was out in the field or the forest or near the ocean. As I read, I noted the things I was already doing that were part of the Wiccan path. For me, all the Wiccan beliefs were already in my heart.

What Wicca Isn't and Never Will be About

As mentioned above, because of the secrecy in Wicca, people have many misconceptions about it. As you now know, Wicca is not about killing or cursing. We do **not** kidnap or abuse others. We do **not** worship Satan or any other demon. And we do **not** hurt or harm anyone or anything, and that includes people, animals, plants, the Earth, and so on. Wiccans believe that everything has a soul. Wiccans respect that soul as a divine part of the Gods and Goddesses.

Don't get me wrong, there is evil out there. If someone calls her/himself a Wiccan and intentionally harms another person, whether it is physical or mental, then that person is **not** truly Wiccan. That person is working against the Craft (shortened from the word Witchcraft.) Also note that true Wiccans follow the local laws and governments where they live.

If you are asked to join a coven that expects you to do things that make you uncomfortable, RUN! If someone says you must have sex with him or her in order to practice the Craft, leave immediately! People who make these demands are manipulating you for their own selfish means. They are **not** practicing perfect love and perfect trust—the cores of the Wiccan faith.

Yes, you may be asked to test some of your boundaries. It can be as simple as sitting with some old pain (such as a past trauma) during a meditation. Personal growth is the focus point. No one should ever pressure you into doing *anything* you are not ready or willing to do freely. Those who do so are **not** following the Wiccan path.

Wiccans Have Nothing to Do with the Devil

Okay, you know it had to come up. Why do a number of people hold the mistaken idea that Witchcraft is connected with Satan or demon worship? Besides the secrecy of Wicca itself, there is another possible explanation. The multiple translations of the *Hebrew Bible* created the biggest problem. When the *Bible* was first translated from the Hebrew and Aramaic into Greek, not all of the words had equivalent word-for-word meanings. For this reason, the meanings of the *Bible's* passages slowly began to change with each different translation.

For an example, let's look at Exodus 22:18. The Hebrew word for "sorcerer, magician, or diviner" was *kashaph*. But when it was translated, it became *Maleficos non patieris vivere*, which is "You shall not permit maleficos to live." Now, Maleficos is a fairly vague term that could mean any kind of criminal. However, the term ultimately became associated with sorcerers during the time of the witch-hunts, which began around the 15th Century and led to the deaths of some 40,000 to 60,000 people (mostly women accused of being witches), often by burning at the stake.

The greatest misfortune for Wicca, with regard to the translation problems of the Bible, occurred when King James I decided to change the translation of the word *Maleficos* into the word "witch." (Note that in Modern English "malefice" means "an evil deed.")

Why did he do that? It was due to his personal hatred of witches. Unfortunately, his actions helped fuel the flames to eradicate all the witches. The view was: "It's in the *Bible*," which meant to the people of the time that the Christian God commanded the killing of witches.

What does this have to do with the Devil? The Hebrews were influential in creating the concept of the Devil. A possible reason for this is the Hebrew belief that evil was caused by an evil spirit, which they called "Satan." The word Satan meant "adversary." When the *New Testament* was translated into Greek, the word became diabolos. The Latin form is *diabolus*, which in English means "devil."

At the time, Satan was still a mostly nebulous concept. But, in later writings, Satan was clearly defined and became an important part of the *New Testament*. It was believed that any spirit entity that wasn't an angel, a saint, or God himself was a demon. This definition of evil spirits was held for all the other Gods, too.

At the time the *New Testament* was written, many people still worshiped the old Gods and didn't have a problem admitting to it. But soon after, the Christians dragged the old Gods through the mud, so to speak, and they became the enemy of the Church.

I have personally spoken to classes of college students studying comparative religion, and I relieved them of the above misunderstandings.

Fear to Tolerance

Powerful fear can be transformed into many things. We'll talk about how fear turns into hate and how we can help resolve this problem.

Why do many people concentrate on differences instead of what we all have in common? Many people hate others based on race, sexual orientation, and religion. These people focus on the differences. Focusing only on differences leads some people to fear. Fear then leads to hate because it's natural to dislike what causes us discomfort.

Many people find Wicca to be quite different from what they call "mainstream faiths" in the western world. Misunderstandings can lead to fear, and that can transform to hate. Unfortunately, people don't ask Wiccans, "What is Wicca all about?"

The problem is that many people take a surface comment from a biased person, and they let that comment give them an impression of Wicca. The biased person does not practice Wicca. To ask that person about Wicca is like asking a plumber to fix your computer.

As children, many people were taught untruths about Wicca. But as adults, they stick with the false stories instead of simply asking a real Wiccan to describe his/her spiritual path.

It's not completely their fault. Life can be hard, and we're all so busy. We often just take a first impression and run with it.

Unfortunately, so much prejudice makes many Wiccans

shy, and they avoid coming out of the "broom closet." A few brave souls step out to speak to the world, but they often run into closed minds and hearts.

The media makes things worse. We know how the media sensationalizes things. News broadcasts feed on creating fear. This in turn generates hate.

So now we have lots of people who hate Wiccans. Much of this hatred could have been avoided.

It may be easy to blame people for their ignorance, but we Wiccans need to move past that. We need to come out of hiding, emerge from the shadows, and share with the world who we are and what we believe.

We believe in harming none. We believe killing is wrong. We believe stealing is wrong, whether it be someone's lunch, car, or spouse. Many of these beliefs compare with the core beliefs of other religions including Judaism, Islam, and Christianity.

We may worship in a different way, but we share similar values. We need to help others and ourselves focus on what unites us so that we can build trust and understanding. Concentrating on our similarities will help dispel hate and bring us all closer together.

How Wiccans Can Handle Stress and Prejudice

We all deal with stress in our lives. However, members of a minority religion face additional stressors. Many Wiccans and Pagans in general have experienced some form of prejudice and some have even been the victims of hate crimes. These and other terrible acts upon us can really take a toll.

Although I am fortunate to live in the San Francisco Bay Area where there is more acceptance of people with differences, I have still faced prejudice. I have lost friendships and suffered the actions of intolerant people.

So how can we combat the stresses of such actions?

First, assess the situation. Can you educate the offending person? I have been in situations when the offending person thinks he's right and will hear nothing that differs from his beliefs.

Make sure no one is being harmed. There is a big difference between offensive words and physical violence. One may need to take action. Maybe you need to quickly get to a place of safety. One might even have to call 911 for police intervention.

Take care of your own feelings. Before I get caught up in an aggression tornado, I remember to simply breathe. Concentrating on your breath is a great way to help yourself calm down. Then you can take control of the words that come out of your mouth. You can't control what they say, but you can control what you say and do.

Find your way to compassion. The Gods and Goddesses love their children (all of them) so become the Goddess in her nurturing state. Let her energy flow within you. Let the Goddess help you select your words. Avoid words that sting, instead say something constructive and nurturing to the conversation. How would this sound? One way to respond is: "I heard what you said. That's *not* what my life is about. I'm leaving this room."

When I say compassion, I do not mean let them walk all over you. The idea is to make space in yourself to understand those who are ignorant of your beliefs. They don't know what they are talking about. To take their words personally gives them power. Do not let that happen. Do *not* give these untruths any power.

Renew yourself. Once the incident is over, take some time

to do a Breathing Meditation. I know how much it helps as a salve to the wounds their words have left.

Find a quiet place where you know you will not be disturbed. Silence your cell phone or home phone. Get comfortable and relax. You can burn some of your favorite incense and light a candle. I find dimming the lights to be helpful.

Here is the process:

As you relax, close your eyes and concentrate on your breathing. Breathing in and out deeply, envision a beautiful white light shining down and surrounding you. Next, deeply breathe in that light, pulling in the beautiful cleansing properties of it. Hold this breath for the count of three.

When you breathe out, picture a black smoke made of those toxic words, actions and emotions. You expel the black smoke from your body. Imagine the black smoke absorbed and purified by the light around you. After your exhalation, hold your breath for a count of three. This is where you acknowledge the transformation of energy.

Continue this process until you feel you have expelled all of the negative comments/feelings/energies that were placed upon you. Finish this meditation by thanking the Gods for their shining light.

May this meditation renew you and free you of any negative effects created by prejudice.

Once free of toxins, you can experience the blessings of life with the Gods and Goddesses.

The Quick Mood Pick-me-up for Wiccans

If the above process doesn't work here are some other options.

A short time before a 4th of July fireworks display was set to start, I sat in a field watching children running, jumping and playing nearby. Their joyful shouts rang in my ears. And an idea arose in my thoughts: *I wish I could just let go like these children and be free from the drudgery of life.*

We all have our moments of sadness, some more than others. Oh to be carefree and happy like a child!

So I came up with the *Quick Mood Pick-me-up for Wiccans*. As some of you may know, I battle depression everyday and these methods can be a lifesaver when in a downer mood. It may not make you as perky and carefree as a happy child, but it will certainly move your mood in a *better direction* to help you get out of a low mood.

Here are *The Quick Mood Pick-me-up for Wiccans* methods:

Lie down in a field of living grass

Laying in grass is relaxing. Further, it's easier for some people to let go when they have more bodily contact with the earth. The process is simple:

Concentrate on the ground beneath you.

Let any negative energy flow from you into the ground. Imagine the ground is a sponge, sucking the negative energy from your body and cleansing the body.

Take deep breaths and let your body relax.

Let Goddess take away all your worries and fears.

Light a candle

If you have racing thoughts, simply light a candle and concentrate on the flame. This can ease your mind.

Cast a circle and place the candle in front of you. You can bless and consecrate it. Make your ritual as simple or as elaborate as you prefer.

Relax and watch the flame.

Breathe slowly and imagine sending your thoughts into the flame to be cleansed from your mind. In this way, you empty your mind of your troubled thoughts.

Hug a tree

I know this must sound a little silly, but hugging a tree is a great way to shunt negative energy into the earth. Any tree will gladly help you.

Wrap your arms around the tree.

Take three deep breaths in and let the tree absorb your negative energy. The tree will do the rest.

Trees naturally shunt energy into the earth. This makes them a great resource for our imbalances in life.

Take a walk in the woods

This is one of the easier practices and it's great exercise. Remember what I shared about trees. In fact just being around trees (and nature) reduces stress. Fear not city dwellers, a park will work just as well. Take deep breaths and relax. Look at your surroundings and see the Gods in all the flowers and trees. Know that you are not alone in your walk, for the Gods walk with you. They support us when no one else can–and even at those times when you might not believe in yourself. The Gods want the best for you.

Talk to a friend

Some people find that they allow being busy to deprive them of actually talking with a friend. Don't let that happen. Talk with a friend and often things appear clearer.

Expressing yourself can wash away the stress and pain of the drudgery of day to day living. If you have a High Priest or Priestess talk to him or her. They are there to support you in your journey. This can be a great bonding experience for both of you.

So if you find yourself in a low mood, remember the *Quick Mood Pick-me-up for Wiccans* methods. I hope they help you as much as they help me.

How to Release Yourself from Self-Judgment

I never expected to be a writer, but the Gods visited me in a dream. I have dyslexia: Writing was the furthest thing from my imagination. In fact, my degrees are in art and web/graphic design.

But the Gods gave me a task: *Write a book for beginners of the Craft that is straightforward and easy to read.*

When I awoke, I felt excited but scared about how I could possibly accomplish this book-writing task. I knew the demands of writing a book because I have close friends who are writers.

How could I possibly write enough to fill a whole book?! It was agony to merely *read* the first book in the *Harry Potter* series due to my dyslexia.

I started to compare myself to other writers by thinking "I'm not a *Scott Cunningham* or a *Starhawk*. What am I *to do*?

I kept thinking about all the other writers of books I had slowly read. Their books were so good. I couldn't match that. The anxiety grabbed me in the chest and I had trouble breathing.

But I strongly believe in the Gods. I know the Gods would not set me up to fail. They love me, and if they say I can do it, *I can.*

The hardest part for me wasn't the task itself, but the constant comparing that I did, placing myself against other writers.

With all of my misspellings, I took blows to my self-esteem each day. My mind raced with negative thoughts of *no one will care about what I have to say; no will read it, and this will never help anyone.*

With all this negativity in my mind, it's a miracle I got anything done. I slowly began to realize something. I cannot compare myself to anyone else. Why? The book I'm writing is a snapshot in time of me. It's about my truth. No one can write it for me.

I was so busy comparing myself to others when in reality there is *no* comparison. There can't be. I am me, no one else, and all those racing thoughts were *not* true.

- Someone will read my book (my editors, for example)
- People will be able to easily read it because my editors will smooth out any rough sections (I love my editors!)
- Someone cares about what I have to say (that someone is *me!*)

My book has already helped someone, *me.*

My book taught me a valuable lesson: *Don't judge or compare yourself to others.*

We all have gifts, different levels of ability. These combinations make us unique and strong. No one else has our particular knowledge and unique set of talents, and this makes each of us *special*.

Comparing my special to your special cannot be done. It's like comparing strawberries and octopi. Because our experiences in life are all slightly or dramatically different (as in different cultures). You just can't compare the two. They are *not* the same.

All I need to do is remember strawberries and octopi.

You're special. Drop comparing yourself to others.

Bring your own special gifts to bear.

The Gods love you and enjoy when you express your creativity.

American Wicca

Many Wiccans feel that the formation of The American Council of Witches in 1973 was one of the best things to happen for Wicca. The Council set common principles that would clarify the pagan and Wiccan religions in North America. Their main goal was to unify and define the many different beliefs of the Wiccan faith. The group also sought to address misinformation about Witchcraft and address the cultural stigma, stereotypes, and lack of governmental recognition. The Council's success is evidenced by the fact that, in 1978, the U.S. Army incorporated the "Thirteen Principles of Wiccan Belief" into its official handbook used by Army chaplains.

Inclusiveness is an important aspect of the Wiccan religion. The doctrine set forth by the American Council of Witches states:

In seeking to be inclusive, we do not wish to open ourselves to the destruction of our group by those on self-serving power trips, or to philosophies and practices contradictory to those principles. In seeking to exclude those whose ways are contradictory to ours, we do not want to deny participation with us to any who are sincerely interested in our knowledge and beliefs, regardless of race, color, sex, age, national or cultural origins, or sexual preference.

The Council worked hard to hammer down the common Beliefs of the Craft, and in so doing, summed up (as best they could) American Wicca. The Principles they established are now the accepted core beliefs of the Craft. Here is the Council's list of Beliefs:

The 13 Principles of the Wiccan Belief:

1. We practice rites to attune ourselves with the natural rhythm of life forces marked by the phases of the Moon and the seasonal Quarters and Cross Quarters.

2. We recognize that our intelligence gives us a unique responsibility towards our environment. We seek to live in harmony with Nature, in ecological balance offering fulfillment to life and consciousness within an evolutionary concept.

3. We acknowledge a depth of power far greater than that is apparent to the average person. Because it is far greater than ordinary it is sometimes called "supernatural", but we see it as lying within that which is naturally potential to all.

4. We conceive of the Creative Power in the universe as manifesting through polarity-as masculine and feminine-and that this same Creative Power lies in all people, and functions through the interaction of the masculine and feminine. We value neither above the other, knowing each to be supportive of the other. We value sex as pleasure, as the symbol and embodiment of life, and as one of the sources of energies used in magickal practice and religious worship.

5. We recognize both outer and inner, or psychological, worlds — sometimes known as the Spiritual World, the Collective Unconscious, Inner Planes, etc. — and we see in the interaction of these two dimensions the basis for paranormal phenomena and magickal exercises. We neglect neither dimension for the other, seeing both as necessary for our fulfillment.

6. We do not recognize any authoritarian hierarchy, but do honor those who teach, respect those who share their greater knowledge and wisdom, and acknowledge

those who have courageously given of themselves in leadership.

7. We see religion, magick and wisdom-in-living as being united in the way one views the world and lives within it — a world view and philosophy of life which we identify as Witchcraft, the Wiccan Way.

8. Calling oneself "Witch" does not make a Witch — but neither does heredity itself, nor the collecting of titles, degrees and initiations. A Witch seeks to control the forces within her/himself that make life possible in order to live wisely and well without harm to others and in harmony with Nature.

9. We believe in the affirmation and fulfillment of life in a continuation of evolution and development of consciousness, that gives meaning to the Universe we know, and our personal role within it.

10. Our only animosity towards Christianity, or toward any other religion or philosophy of life, is to the extent that its institutions have claimed to be "the only way," and have sought to deny freedom to others and to suppress other ways of religious practice and belief.

11. As American Witches, we are not threatened by debates on the history of the Craft, the origins of various terms, the origins of various

aspects of different traditions. We are concerned with our present and our future.

12. We do not accept the concept of absolute evil, nor do we worship any entity known as "Satan" or "the Devil", as defined by Christian tradition. We do not seek power through the suffering of others, nor do we accept that personal benefit can be derived only by denial to another.

13. We believe that we should seek within Nature that which is contributory to our health and well-being.

Another view of Wicca comes from The Covenant of the Goddess, a cross-traditional Wiccan group with over 100 affiliated covens. This viewpoint has great meaning to me because I am a priestess and a member of the Covenant of the Goddess.

Founded in 1975, this group seeks to increase cooperation among Witches and secure the legal protection enjoyed by members of other faiths. According to their website (www.cog.org):

> The Covenant of the Goddess is one of the largest and oldest Wiccan religious organizations. Wicca, or Witchcraft is the most popular expression of the religious movement known as Neo-Paganism. Wicca or Witchcraft is the fastest growing religion in the United States according to the Institute for the Study of

American Religion. Its practitioners are reviving ancient Pagan practices and beliefs of pre-Christian Europe and adapting them to contemporary life. The result is a religion that is both old and new, both traditional and creative.

The Covenant of the Goddess has this to say:

Wicca, or Witchcraft, is an earth religion — a re-linking (re-ligio) with the life-force of nature, both on this planet and in the stars and space beyond. In city apartments, in suburban backyards, in country glades, groups of women and men meet on the new and full moons and at festival times to raise energy and put themselves in tune with these natural forces. They honor the old Goddesses and Gods, including the Triple Goddess of the waxing, full, and waning moon, and the Horned God of the sun and animal life, as visualizations of immanent nature. Our religion is not a series of precepts or beliefs, rather we believe that we each have within ourselves the capacity to reach out and experience the mystery — that feeling of ineffable oneness with all Life. Those who wish to experience this transcendence must work, and create, and participate in their individual religious lives. For this reason, our congregations, called covens, are small groups which give room for each individual to contribute to the efforts of the group by self-knowledge and creative experimentation within the agreed-upon group structure or tradition. There are many traditions or sects within the Craft. Different groups take their inspiration from the pre-Christian religions of certain ethnic groups (e.g. Celtic, Greek, Norse, Finno-Ugric); in the liturgical works of some modern Witch poet or scholar (e.g. Gerald Gardner, Z Budapest, Alex Sanders, Starhawk); or by seeking within themselves for inspiration and direction. Many feminists have turned to Wicca and the role of priestess for healing and strength after the patriarchal oppression and lack of voice for women in the major world religions. There are many paths to spiritual growth. Wicca is a participatory revelation, a celebratory action leading to greater understanding of oneself and the universe. We believe there is much to learn by studying our past, through myth, through ritual drama, through poetry and music, through love and through living in harmony with the Earth.

Magick: the White / Black of it

Magick is a *natural* power, not a supernatural one. When Wiccans do magick, they channel natural energies and create change with them.

Please note that there is no such thing as black or white witches. Many people incorrectly believe that "black" witches perform bad or evil magick and "white" witches only do good magick.

For the sake of this discussion, think of magick like a

knife. A knife can take a life or, in a surgeon's skilled hands, can save a life. The same is true with magick, which is a combination of energy and knowledge. Energy like electricity can be used for anything depending on the appliance you plug in and how you use it. You can plug in a toaster or a power saw. And both can hurt you if you're not careful.

Wiccans use magick to heal. That's putting it simply and clearly. Often, Wiccans use magick to enhance the body's natural healing tendencies.

Black Mass

This drives me crazy. So many people think witches do black masses. That is simply not true. The Black Mass was *never* a part of Witchcraft. Let me repeat: Wiccans do **NOT** do Black Masses—never have, never will.

The Black Mass is a part of the history of Christianity, and Wicca predates Christianity. Therefore, it doesn't make sense for Wicca to have any connection to any so-called Black Masses.

There is only one documented historical case of a Black Mass which was performed by an ordained Catholic priest during the reign of Louis the XIV, known as the Sun King. Louis' mistress had engaged the Catholic priest in the attempt to force Louis to abandon his new lover. The police investigated the case, and arrests were made.

If you look at the actual sources of what is now called the Black Mass, you can see how ludicrous it is to connect Wicca to any of it. Finally, other reports continue to associate defrocked *Christian* priests with Black Masses.

So...what does all this have to do with Wicca? Real Witchcraft had nothing to do with these so-called Black

Mass events and yet Wicca got blamed for them—a pattern of blame that would be repeated throughout history.

So How Can Wicca Help Me?

Okay, so Wicca isn't the big bad scary thing some people think it is. Witches don't really have supernatural powers (sorry to burst your bubble).

But wait a minute. Didn't I say earlier that Wiccans can do magick? Yes, I did, and that is true. However, the ability to do magick is a *natural* power, not a supernatural one. When we do magick, we channel natural energies and create change with them.

Well, if Witchcraft isn't really supernatural, then why practice Wicca at all? Why not follow another spiritual path? It would certainly be easier to go with a mainstream religion. You wouldn't get the dirty looks and the 'baby-eater' accusations that are so often directed at Wiccans. Why practice any religion for that matter?

Everyone is different and has their own answer to that question. I like to think of religion as a bottle of wine. Let's say you have three different people who all taste the same bottle of wine. The first person points out that the flavor has accents of oak. The second praises the hints of apple in it, and the third enjoys the floral notes. They are all right. The wine contains all the flavors they described. But each person detected something different. Religion is like that. Deity can't be entirely known. So the truth of it is scattered into many faiths.

I love nature, and I enjoy these "notes" of the wine. The beauties and wonders of nature surround me. Other paths require that you must go somewhere to be with Deity—a mosque, a church, or another particular place where you go to God. This doesn't work for me.

On the other hand, with Wicca, the Gods are not only everywhere and all around me at all times, but they are within me as well. I am never without my Gods. And they come to circle often when asked.

That's right, your eyes didn't deceive you in that last paragraph. I am literally the Goddess and God, and these Gods don't judge me! They support me, love me, and help me just for who I am, not for what I look like. I don't need to change or alter myself to be loved. No diets or creams are required. The best thing about all this spiritual yumminess is that it's all part of the natural world. That's the thing I love most. The Gods are of the trees, the birds, the stag, the Earth itself.

The natural world is what I live in, and it is my reality. I'm not trying to get to some euphoric place I've never experienced. I'm not trying to jump impossible hurdles with rules that can never truly be successfully followed. All I must do is be me. That's it.

We are rewarded with love and kindness when we give love and kindness. What we put out into the universe, the universe gives us back threefold. (Remember the Universal Pond.) This cycle, among all the others, is all natural. Angry, vengeful god, *not* included! And that's the way I like it.

So now that we know what Wicca is, the real question is: "How can Wicca help me?"

I'll share my story. Finding the Gods was a lifesaver, literally. Before I had the Gods in my life, I was a kid with huge self-esteem problems. I had made multiple suicide attempts.

When I was eight, I was so depressed about my life that I tied a string around my neck, intending to hang myself. But the Gods were on my side even then. The string broke. The

Gods knew I had a purpose; I had work to do for them. But at that time I could only think, "I'm so lame, I can't even kill myself right!" I couldn't see it for the blessing that it was. I just fell into a deeper depression. There were other attempts, and luckily, other failures.

My childhood was filled with physical and mental torture perpetrated by my older brother—and my parents' neglect. Somehow I survived to my sixteenth year.

One day, I walked into a Barnes and Noble bookstore in my hometown. Earlier that year, I had heard a new word, *Wicca*, so I asked the sales clerk, "Do you have any books on Wicca?" Her eyes lit up, and with great excitement she led me to a shelf and started pouring books into my arms.

That evening, alone in my room, I started to read Scott Cunningham's book, *Wicca: A Guide for the Solitary Practitioner*. My heart filled up. I had finally found my home.

Now I reveled in a new world. Soon I was meditating, and after some sessions, the Gods made contact with me.

The Gods embraced me with pure love. My body filled up with their love for me. It moved from my head through my entire body, down to my fingers and toes. Happiness was so foreign to me; I had never felt this way before. But I shifted to a deep part of myself I hadn't known, where I knew that I was one with the Gods. Forever.

The Gods found me beautiful. They took pride in me.

I never knew anyone could have this much love for anyone, especially me! This epiphany was a brilliant light into my chasm of darkness and despair. Now I could start to see myself for what I really was worth.

With this knowledge, I found a new confidence in life. Once the Gods opened me up and shone their loving light in me, I was transformed into love—love for myself and for others.

The "harm none" concept of Wicca rang true for me. I didn't want anyone to go through what I had endured. I wanted to treat everyone with respect, compassion, and love. So I started on my path and became a Wiccan priestess.

It's a beautiful path.

I want to emphasize that the "An it harm none" concept (The Wiccan Rede) not only applied to not hurting others, but it also included *not hurting myself.*

Before I connected with the Gods and Goddesses, I believed that I wasn't worth the dirt I stood on. At that time I was so sure of it!

Then, I met the Gods. What they showed me didn't match what certain people had been showing me my whole life. My brother called me "Piggy," although I weighed only 112 pounds at the time. I later learned that he was full of garbage. The Gods showed me that I was made perfect, even if the world around me called me broken. I chose to believe in the love of the Gods.

I discovered that magazines that tell me I'm too fat and not beautiful enough are liars! I don't have to be a size 0 to be beautiful and happy. I don't have to use their creams and gels to improve my looks. I just have to be me. With the Gods' help, I can better see the world. I can see situations more clearly and more positively.

The Freedom of Wicca

Choosing the Wiccan path is choosing freedom. Why? Here are a number of details that reveal various levels of freedom.

Wiccans can choose who they practice with. I don't just mean the people next to you, but you also get to choose which Gods you worship. Wiccans can choose the Egyptian pantheon of Gods or *not!* If Osiris isn't the God for you, pick another deity. This is very important to us as Wiccans. Most Wiccans have enjoyed choosing a particular patron deity. This is a personal decision. I have Cernunnos as mine. Worshiping *your* Gods is much more important than worshiping someone else's. You're not boxed into following what someone else believes. No one tells us who we can and can't worship. It's one of the main freedoms that I cherish the most.

We are the captains of our own "ships of belief." In other religions one must conform to what the leaders tell you to believe and what they tell you to do. Some religions enforce that people gather on certain days of the week and must hear a certain person give a speech. On the other hand, Wiccans can choose which rituals they perform and when. They can choose to celebrate a ritual as a solitary practitioner or they can join a coven.

We all have our own paths to walk with the freedom to walk with or without certain companions. Sometimes we follow someone else's footsteps for a while, so we may learn the Craft. Then, we have the freedom to move on. Each of us is on an individual path. Sometimes our path lines up with someone else's path. This is great because you can travel together and learn from one another. Then, when you heart tells you, you are free to separate and continue on your own path in a different direction.

Wicca does not force you to stay in life-long relationships. Wicca emphasizes "as long as love shall last" so one is not forced to remain married. Your individual path is respected.

Wicca does not force practitioners to practice intolerance. For example, a number of religions tell their practitioners that gays are an abomination and an angry, vengeful God will punish them. Instead, Wiccans love all representations of the

Gods. No one is an abomination because of the way they were born. We were made the way we are by the Gods on purpose, and they made each and every one of us with great love and care. Black, white, gay, straight, we are all beautiful the way we are. To hate those differences is to hate the Gods' work.

As Wiccans we have the freedom to practice what and how we want. We have the freedom to practice when and with whom we want. There are no strings attached. There is nothing to bind our hands and feet when it comes to our own personal practice. Wicca is full of the freedom to choose. We can see it in our practices. No wonder Wicca is one of the fastest growing faiths in the world.

Reasons to Choose Wicca

Besides making a positive psychological impact, Wicca can also help you live a healthier life. From revering the outdoors and nature to holding the body sacred, Wicca can give you peace. Here are some of my reasons for embracing the Wiccan faith:

1) Wicca embraces meditation, which is good for your mental health.

Meditation . . .
- calms the mind.
- reduces stress
- allows you to explore, learn about yourself, and communicate with the Gods

Meditation helps us to delve into our subconscious mind. Meditation is also a great way to meet and talk with Deity.

2) Wicca is good for your physical health.

You take care of your "your body temple." You can dance in ritual and enjoy nature hikes.

Physical health is vital for several reasons. Having a well tuned body generates more power. This helps in doing our Craft. Dancing and regular exercise is one way to honor the Gods—for our bodies truly are temples.

3) Being out in Nature has health benefits all its own.

Taking walks in nature helps keep our temple operating at its peak. And such walks take us into the natural places that the Gods created for us to enjoy. It gives us great joy to feel one with the natural world. While out in the abundance of nature, we can attune ourselves to the rhythms of the Earth and come closer to the Gods and our own true nature.

4) Wicca is good for your spirit.

Communicating with the Gods gives us the close bond we desire to have with them. The Gods are our teachers. They help us to understand ourselves and the world around us. They teach us how to grow spiritually and give us feedback through our intuition. Their cycles teach us about death and rebirth. We see ourselves in and part of that cycle, too.

Furthermore, we learn about where we go when we die. For many Wiccans, we go to the Summerlands. This is a place of rest and renewal where we look over our recent incarnation and decide whether to return to the earth in a new incarnation. Going through multiple lifetimes helps us learn and become closer to the God and Goddess.

A life-affirming religion, Wicca helps you explore many things about life and death. Now, through this book, I trust that your view of Wicca is expanding. Wicca is about faith in the God and Goddess and personal growth. It is a path of peace and love.

What We Think Will Make Us Happy

As a young girl I fantasized about someone who would rescue me from the horrible conditions of my home life. My brother terrorized me and almost killed me by holding me underwater in a neighbor's pool. He was 12 and I was 8.

As I did chores around the house, I fantasized that someone at any moment would come in and take me away from my terrible situation.

When I got a little older I met a guy who I thought could solve my plight. If we just could get married, we'd be independent. I'd finally be out of the house and I would be happy. No more mental, verbal and physical abuse. This was the chance I was waiting for.

So at 18, I married him. Things seemed fine at first. We got a place of our own and I went to school and "Joe" went to work. At the time I was studying to be a computer animator.

At first, Joe said a few things that felt cruel. I just thought he was having an occasional bad day. But it became more frequent.

Joe had control of the money accounts. I said we needed to buy groceries. "Too expensive," he said. But while he was out, he'd eat at restaurants, leaving me with empty cupboards and nothing to eat. So often I felt hungry.

Then in the evening, he'd take me to fast food restaurants. My body began to live in starvation mode. Soon when I ate, my body clung to every calorie.

With no food in the daytime, and fast food (no vegetables) at night, I started gaining weight. Then Joe berated me for the changes in my body. His verbal abuse beat down my soul.

Was it all his fault that this had happened to me? No. It was *my* fault. I was so desperate for someone else to solve my problems that I didn't stop and ask the Gods what I should do.

Once I reached out to the Gods, they opened my eyes. I needed to save myself.

No, I do *not* excuse my ex-husband's behavior. But I learned that I needed to stand up for myself. I initiated divorce proceedings.

With the Gods' guidance, I learned that it's my responsibility to make me happy. Now whenever I face dilemmas I bring them to the Gods' for guidance.

I've learned that true happiness can vary greatly from fantasies. I've also learned that when I take responsibility to face the truth of my situation and I take positive action the Gods smile upon my efforts.

My life has steadily improved by listening to the Gods' counsel.

So the next time you are stumped with life problems, talk to the Gods. Perhaps, take a walk and watch for signs in the world around you.

Maybe you'll gaze upon the full moon and ask the Goddess for her advice.

Realize that some Wiccans do not hear the Gods' voices directly. They just feel a *quickening of their intuition*.

Knowing the Gods are there for me brings me great comfort.

May you know the blessings of the Gods.

Chapter Questions

1. What is The Law of Three?
2. What is The Wiccan Rede?
3. Why were witches *mistakenly* thought to have been Satan worshipers?
4. What do Wiccans attune themselves to?

CHAPTER 2:
THE HISTORY

To truly understand Wicca, we need to look at its roots. Looking at Witchcraft through a historical perspective will help eliminate many of the misconceptions that people of other faiths hold about Wicca.

Witchcraft began in Africa, spread throughout the Mediterranean, then expanded into northern Europe where it evolved over time. Wiccan practices can be traced back to the ancient past of those areas.

An example of a Wiccan practice is shown in cave paintings in Europe. These paintings date from the Stone Age period and depict a ritual in which the participants wore masks and horns.

When early humans first began to ponder the existence of the God and Goddess, they looked to the natural world as their guide. Our ancestors worshiped the God of hunting and the Goddess of fertility. They viewed the God as the hunter and the protector—virile loving, and strong. They saw him as the rutting stag, the fertilizing rain, the lightning bolt, and the impressive great oak. The God supported the Goddess and loved her.

The Goddess's role in nature was to teach and protect her children, much like a mother bear protects her cubs. The Goddess suckles humankind at her breast, providing the ripe harvest of the land to feed and nourish them. She gives birth to all things. People see the nurturing Goddess in caves, flowers, rivers, the wind, and the Earth.

The Burning Times

People worshiped the Gods openly and freely until the Burning Times, also known as the Witch Craze or the Inquisition, which lasted for more than 300 years, from about 1480 to 1750. Historians debate the number of people murdered (accused of Witchcraft) during this time. Most agree the number is between 40,000 to 50,000, although some put it around 100,000.

In 1480, the Spanish Inquisition was started by Queen Isabella I of Castile and King Ferdinand II of Aragon, who fought to maintain Catholic orthodoxy in their kingdoms. They demanded that Jews and Muslims convert to Christianity or leave. Another purpose of the Spanish Inquisition was to root out Witchcraft.

By 1487, the Burning Times was in full swing. In the same year the *Malleus Maleficarum*, or *The Hammer of the Witches*, was written. The Hammer of the Witches gave inquisitors step-by-step instructions on how to find a witch, how to elicit a confession (almost always by torture), and how to convict them. At no time was a witch considered innocent.

Due to the misogyny that was rampant in Europe at the time, the *Mallus Maleficarum* said, "ALTHOUGH far more women are witches than men, as was shown in the First Part of the work, yet men are more often bewitched than women. And the reason for this lies in the fact that GOD allows the devil more power over the venereal act, by which the original sin is handed down, than over other human actions." Remember, the quote "GOD allows the devil more power over the venereal act" because many Christians don't honor sex as sacred.

Because of this wording, most if not all women were suspected of being witches. The authors felt that the female gender was inherently weaker and thus more susceptible to demonic temptations. Most of those accused were widows or older women who lived on the fringes of society and who didn't have male protection from a husband, brother, or son. This is one of the things that deeply angers me about the Burning Times. Here we have a society that is sick—that is against women and against sexuality. And what does this society do? It murders people over this!

But it was King James VI of Scotland (before he became King James I of England and Ireland) who ushered in the peak period of the Burning Times. A series of fateful events brought Witchcraft to the forefront of James' mind. The first occurred in 1589 when a trip to bring Anne of Denmark, his bride, to Scotland turned into a terrible ordeal. Windstorms whipped the ship so badly that the ship's commander claimed Witchcraft had something to do with it. The ship turned back, causing James to set sail for Copenhagen later that year to get married. The couple's return trip was also beset by terrible storms. While in Denmark, a country persecuting witches, James studied Witchcraft as a branch of theology.

Then, in 1590, James VI attended the North Berwick Witch Trials. This was the first major persecution of witches in Scotland under the English Witchcraft Act of 1563.. During the two-year period of the trials, 70 people were convicted of using Witchcraft to send storms against James' ship—a treasonous act. James became obsessed with the threats supposedly from witches and personally supervised the torture of the accused. His experience with the trials led him in 1597 to write *Daemonologie,* a book that supported witch hunting. (Note that he also changed the *Bible.* The King James version was published about 15 years later.)

Before the North Berwick Witch Trials, Witchcraft was seen as heresy. At the time Witchcraft was seen as a competing religion with the Catholic faith. Witches had to be practicing Christians before they could be condemned. During this time the rulers Queen Isabella and King Ferdinand had won a war against the Islamic Moors and had driven them out of Spain in 1492. Queen Isabella and King Ferdinand required everyone to convert to Catholicism, thereby expelling practicing Muslims and Jews. Anyone wishing to remain had to convert so pagans kept their practices covertly. (Before forced conversions, pagans had been protected under Muslim laws in Spain).

But now it was seen as a crime against God himself. It was at this time that the laws began to equate the old pagan Gods with evil spirits and demons, and thus accused witches as devil worshipers. After all, witches had gone after the King. They needed to be eradicated!

James, as the King of Scots, maintained his stance against Witchcraft until he was crowned James I of England and Ireland. The English court had never accepted the Christian witch theory of demonic behavior. After his ascension, James quickly ditched his views on the issue. Since Witchcraft was not a topic usually included in British intellectual discourse, James felt that association with the topic would be a potential embarrassment. Witch trials did occur in England under his rule, although they occurred less often than in Spain. It was the press coverage of the day that led people to believe that they were more common than they actually were.

Certain Christians Hold False Beliefs about "A Pact with Satan"

Between the 14th and 18th centuries, the Burning Times continued throughout the rest of Europe. Christians *mistakenly* believed that witches made pacts with Satan. As I mentioned earlier, Wiccans have nothing to do with Satan or any demon. Besides, Satan is a Judeo-Christian idea.

Nevertheless, the mistaken Christians used these false and "suspected pacts" as a tool to improperly prosecute witches. The court trials distinguished between a person who was possessed by Satan against his/her will and a person who willingly made a pact with Satan and thus consciously went against God. Christians also accused witches of having sexual orgies, sacrificing men and children, and eating babies. These *horrible and false allegations* were "the same old, false stuff" that had been used against other groups in the past. For example, the Syrians accused the Jews of these same crimes; the Romans charged the Christians with the same atrocities; the Christians made the same accusations against the witches. And in modern times, the Nazis accused the Jews of eating babies at their Friday Sabbats.

The consequence of being charged with Witchcraft was usually torture, the main tool for interrogation. Some of the devices used included thumbscrews, whipping stocks, scalding lime baths, and the rack. During their torture, the accused would be asked a standard list of questions. The intense pain would force many to confess to whatever their torturers asked, no matter how bizarre. The confession would generally be enough for a conviction. Often the torturer would demand to know the names of other witches, and that led to more arrests, torture, and convictions. Thus the cycle fed upon itself, expanding into an ever-growing spiral.

The Burning Times continued raging until the 1700s when they finally began to fade. Some scholars suggest that the atrocities of several controversial trials eventually led to a quieting of mass hysteria and even a turn in public opinion. Such horrible trials included the witch trials of Mora, Sweden (1668-1676) that led to the execution of 70 adults and 15 children, and the trails in Salem, Massachusetts (1692-1693) that led to the deaths of 25 people. Eventually the Church issued a statement that it was a heresy to believe in the existence of witches, and that witchcraft itself never existed and was only a delusion in people's minds. This was a *change* from a century before when the Church punished people for the heresy of believing that witches *did not* exist.

Eventually, stories about witches were considered old wives' tales that were retold to scare children.

We may imagine that persecution of witches for the most part ended in the 1700s, but let's notice that The Witchcraft laws continued in England until 1951. That year the Witchcraft laws were replaced with the Fraudulent Mediums Act, which was next repealed in 2008 and replaced with the Consumer Protection Regulation in the European Union (EU).

In Conclusion

We have examined the history of Witchcraft and seen the misconceptions that raged though centuries. Popular opinion has been hard on witches and the Wicca faith, and that *negative bias is still present*. But today's witches are trying hard to shed light on the misinformation and turn the discussion to a more enlightened and intelligent discourse. Wicca is growing fast and is becoming very popular with those who dare to seek the truth.

Chapter Questions

1. How long did the Burning Times last?
2. Explain why Christians falsely believed Witches made a pact with Satan?
3. When was the *Malleus Maleficarum,* or *The Hammer of the Witches,* written?

CHAPTER 3:
WHO ARE THE GOD AND THE GODDESS?

As a young girl, I was shy. I'm not talking about being just a little quiet. I was so shy I couldn't even talk to people. It's no surprise that my sense of self-worth was nonexistent!

This left the door wide open for bullies and the like. I was teased and tormented mercilessly. Day in and day out, the torment never stopped. Yet, the worst place for me was at home.

Home was supposed to be a safe place, but mine wasn't. My brother, three years older and much bigger than me, used to beat me. He once held me underwater in a swimming pool at a friend's house. He finally let go when I stopped struggling.

My parents didn't do a thing to stop my brother's abuse, even when the abuse was done blatantly in front of them. This was a huge hit to my sense of self-worth. I thought, "If my own parents don't think I'm worth saving, then I must be not worth anything."

As I grew up, these messages continued to grip my

reality. I was alone against a heartless world. I was beyond miserable.

Then I found the Gods. The first book I read about the Craft was like a breath of fresh air to someone who had been suffocating for years. I had finally found something that spoke the truth to me. As I continued to read more and more books, it hit me: "Goddess doesn't make crap!" What this meant to me was that I had value. The truth was the complete opposite of what I had always thought. I found that I was unique and special to the Gods, and I was exactly as I had been created to be. If the Gods loved me for being who I was, then I could love me, too! And I was worth standing up for!

At first, people got mad when I stood up for myself. But after a while, they did start to treat me with more respect. Not everyone changed, but that's their loss. I am a beautiful, loving person. No one deserves to be treated the way I had been treated. It was just wrong. And it's not the way the Gods want us to treat one another.

The Gods love us all. We are all unique, and that makes us special. This is the truth no matter what anyone says.

So Why Does Pain Exist?

Many people of various faiths have wondered why Deity lets pain exist. Why do we have to go through such pain? I'm not talking about only one kind of pain. I am talking about all kinds of pain that we endure—from the physical pain of skinning a knee to the emotional pain of losing a loved one.

It certainly isn't a happy experience. So why? Why do the Gods let us—no, need us—to experience it?

Simply, it is used as a teaching tool. Understand that the Gods do not inflict this upon us. We do it to ourselves. Not intentionally, of course. We don't want to skin our knees when we fall; it is just the way of life.

During our lives we learn lessons; some are truly painful. The more painful the lesson, the more we tend to remember the lesson. Learning to walk or ride a bicycle involves falling. But we get up again. If you skin your knee, you're motivated to do better at staying upright. Pain motivates us to do better.

Emotional pain teaches us different things. If someone makes fun of you, you're likely to have hurt feelings. For many of us, this pain teaches us to avoid taunting others. (Remember the Law of Three!)

Okay you say: "What about the death of a loved one? What does that teach us?"

The trauma caused by the death of a loved one can teach us a number of lessons. I mostly focus on two: loss and love.

When you experience the loss of someone you loved, you understand how much the person meant to you. This is one way you know that you truly loved someone. This can be love for a friend, a parent, or a lover/spouse. With the loss, you can now understand love completely.

As hard and unforgiving as pain is, we still need it to help us learn and therefore grow. Without it, we can't experience true compassion, trust, and love.

Let's Talk about the Gods

So where, who, and what are the Gods? Well, for starters, the Gods are immanent in all things. This means that they dwell within all things. The Gods are a part of you and me. They are the air we breathe, the food we eat, and the water we drink. They are within and all around everything and everyone visible and invisible. Many religions think that "God" is somewhere *out there*, separate from human beings. Wiccans believe that the old Gods and Goddesses are in us and in all things. (By "old Gods and Goddesses," I'm referring to Zeus, Pan, Diana, Astarte, and others.)

Whether you are male or female, you have both the God and the Goddess within you now. Masculine and feminine energies are found within each of us. Some scholars refer to the animus (male energy) and anima (female energy). The yin/yang symbol is a great representation of this.

Let's dig deeper into discussing the God and Goddess of Witchcraft. Let's start with the big picture. The "All" encompasses both masculine and feminine into one in Wicca. For example, think of the All as a large faceted gem. You see that half of the gem is green (the color of the Goddess) and the other half is red (the color of the god). Both the green and the red sides are needed to make the whole gem, which is the "All," the whole of deity.

Each side of the gem has a role. Looking at this two-toned gem as a whole, you can see that both the red and green sides have innumerable facets. The green side represents the Goddess, and the red side represents the God. Let's look at the red side or God side of the gem first.

Each of the many facets on the red side (the God or masculine side) of the "All" gem represents a different face of the God. Each of these facets represents a different aspect of the god, and each has different attributes and abilities. For example, Osiris, Pan, and Zeus each have their own facet on the red side.

The green side, or the Goddess side of the gem, also has innumerable facets, and these represent the feminine aspect of the All. Just like the God side of the gem, the green side's facets are the many different faces of the Goddess. Again each facet is a completely unique Goddess. For example, Diana, Hecate, and Bridget each have their own facet. Combined, all the Goddesses create the whole of femininity, and therefore, the whole of the Goddess.

You need both halves, the green (the Goddess) and the red (the God) to make a whole gem that represents the All. In other words, all of the Gods and Goddesses need to be present to create a complete Deity (or the whole gem), and the All encompasses this wholeness of deity.

So, in summary, all of the Gods make up the complete masculine and all of the Goddesses make up the complete feminine. With the complete masculine and complete feminine, we have the All, which has the totality of the Gods and Goddesses as one.

The Many Faces of Deity

Each of us has a unique understanding of Deity. We see Deity as a reflection of ourselves. But since we can't understand the entire whole of Deity at once, the Gods come to us in ways we can comprehend. They show themselves to us as facets or slices of themselves so that we can relate to them. One person's understanding of Deity is likely to be quite different than someone else's. Too much for anyone to truly understand, Deity (or the All) stands as our guide and shows us the way. At this time we are not evolved enough, in this incarnation, to see and know the whole picture and truth of the All. But we can see slices or facets of the All, and all of these slices add up to complete the picture of the whole. Here's another way to look at it: We can have a single drop of the Pacific Ocean and know that it represents and comes from the whole of the ocean, but we can't possibly see or comprehend the ocean in its entirety. The ocean is too vast a concept.

Because of this, not only does each person see Deity in his or her own way, but each culture sees Deity in its own way, too. It's just like the story of the blind men and the elephant:

> A number of blind men came to an elephant. Somebody told them that it was an elephant. The blind men asked, 'What is the elephant like?' and they began to touch its body. One of them said: 'It is like a pillar.' This blind man had only touched its leg. Another man said, 'The elephant is like a husking basket.' This person had only touched its ears. Similarly, he who touched its trunk or its belly talked of it differently. In the same way, he who has seen the Lord in a particular way limits the Lord to that alone and thinks that He is nothing else.

- Mahendranath Gupta, 1883

This fable reminds us that we each see Deity differently, and that each person's understanding of Deity is correct for them.

The Creation Myth

In many cultures, the myths of the creation of the Goddess and God follow a common pattern. Wiccans believe that the Goddess created herself and then, in an expression of love and ecstasy, split herself and gave birth to the God. This produced the first polarity. The new couple then created all manifestations of life and matter through their continued ecstasy. Here is how I express it:

In the beginning there was nothing but the Void. Then, with a single thought of "I AM!" the All created itself. But soon, the All got lonely and so separated itself into two. The All did this by making a mighty scream. The Dark half became the Goddess. She in turn gave birth to the other half of herself. A new entity was created. At first this entity was only a wave, but soon, it had thought, and so became illumination. With illumination the entity became intelligent; he was the God, the Light half to the Goddess. God slowly continued to drift away from the Goddess. Soon after his illumination God realized he had been created. He was curious about who had created him and so turned and started to make a circle, looking for the one who had made him. Searching in an entire circle, he realized that his creator was not anywhere he had looked. So the only place his creator could be was in the center of the circle. So he went there, where he met the Goddess.

The God was brilliant and irresistible to the Goddess. The Goddess fell in love with the God, for he was radiant beyond compare, and so she made love to him and, in ecstasy, they created all we know.

Remember this story can be interpreted in many different ways, and many cultures have their own interpretations.

The Goddess

The Goddess has many names: Diana, Aphrodite, Arianrhod, Ceridwen, Demeter, and so on. Numerous books have been written about the Goddess and her many-faceted depictions. In this section we will study the main attributes of the Goddess as a whole without focusing on any single story or cultural interpretation of her. (See the Appendix with the reading list for additional materials.) For now we will look at the basic cycles she exhibits and how they relate to nature and our lives.

Early humans recognized the first deity as the Goddess. The first known representation of the Goddess dates from the Paleolithic period. In December 1994, Jean Culottes discovered the Chauvet caves in the Ardéche valley in southern France. The Chauvet cave's paintings are in such good condition that at first researchers thought it was a hoax. So they tested the paintings with carbon dating and discovered that the paintings were apparently completed some 32,000 years ago. Some of the art was carbon dated as 5,000 years apart from other artwork in the same caves. We realize that during some of this time period Neanderthals still roamed the lands.

The reason these cave paintings are in such good condition was the fact that the entrance of the cave collapsed sealing off the cave creating, in effect, a time capsule preserving all the paintings within.

In "the Chambers of the Lions," the researchers have found the earliest depiction of a human being known to exist. It is a stalactite made to represent the genitalia of a human female with the head of a bison.

As a mixed figure, this implies some form of Deity. Perhaps, human beings encountered Deity at that time.

Found near the village of Willendorf in Austria, a sculpture called the Venus of Willendorf was carved sometime between 24,000 and 22,000 BC. It depicts the Goddess with a large swollen belly, full breasts, and large buttocks. Thought to have been an exaggerated symbol for women's fertility.

Because woman gave birth, she held the mysteries of life. Woman was the Goddess in flesh, and so she was respected in early history. The Goddess represents fertility itself, for human, beast, and bud alike. The mighty creatrix, the Goddess, gives birth to all we see. Both the giver and receiver of life, she has the ever-fertile womb of life, and her cauldron is the receiver of the dead. Witches see the cauldron as a symbol of reincarnation. Only through the Goddess's cauldron can the dead be reborn.

The Goddess has two sides: the light mother and the dark mother. You can't have one without the other. Both the creator (the light side) and the destroyer (the dark side), she makes way for new life to grow. Just as fertility creates the rose, she must wither the rose and take it back within herself to provide nourishment for others. Both sides of the Goddess, the light and the dark, are needed. Without both, there can't be a whole.

The light side of the Goddess represents the awake and conscious part of our minds. The dark half of the Goddess represents our unconscious minds. The Goddess symbolizes both sides of the human psyche.

The dark side of the Goddess can be frightening. Representing our Shadow Self and the unconscious, she encompasses the dark side of our personality. This part of us conceals our negative thoughts and emotions. We do not always like or acknowledge this part of our being, but without it we would not be who we are.

Just like the Goddess, we need both the dark and light sides of ourselves to be whole. We need both the unconscious and the conscious. When we sleep, our dreams can be positive or frightening nightmares. Both the positive dream and the nightmare become keys to truth, and therefore, lead to growth. They both open doors to insight into ourselves.

Aspects of The Goddess

The Goddess has many symbols to represent her, one of the most prominent being the moon. The phases of the moon not only, in effect, reenact the menses of the Goddess and of all women each month, but they also represent the three aspects of the Goddess: Maiden, Mother, and Crone. These show the life cycle of the Goddess and all living beings. This reflects the phases of our life: birth, the fertile adult, and the maturity of old age to death.

1. The young virgin, represented by *The Maiden*.
2. The fertile bringer of life and nurturing aspect of the Goddess, represented by *The Mother*.
3. The mature, wise woman as well as the destructive aspect of the Goddess, represented by *The Crone*.

The waxing moon represents the Maid aspect of the Goddess. As the fertile virgin, The Maid, also known as the young maiden, waits to be impregnated by her other half — the God. Courted by the God, she is to produce all that's needed for our sustenance: animals, the harvests, and humankind. She can be seen as the seductress, the sexual lover of the God. Her fertility facilitates this seduction, with the blessing of the creation of all. During the springtime, the budding flower represents The Maiden aspect of the Goddess. The Maiden flourishes during this time of the year, and in so doing, attracts the God.

The full moon represents the Mother aspect of the Goddess. Characterized by the full belly of pregnancy, the Goddess symbolizes the fullness of nature's bounty. She is seen as the nurturing Earth Mother, creating sustenance for life, taking her place as the fertile and mature consort to the God. She is mother to all and from whence all life springs forth. She rules at midsummer, the height of her fertility. She teaches, represented as the loving mother who guides those who seek the light and blessings of motherhood. The Goddess, standing for the endless bounty of the Earth, has as her symbol the ripe fruit of the Earth. She provides for all her children and uses love and compassion to guide them.

The dark or waning moon represents the Crone aspect of the Goddess. The mature and wise councilor, the Crone has seen and done it all before. She has been the Maiden, and she has been the Mother, and now she has the wisdom of the Crone. She advises the God, who listens to her sage advice. She uses her symbol, the scythe, to reap the land of the old to make way for the new.

The Crone gives rest to what had once been given life. Once we return to her cauldron, we wait to be reborn. She takes the body back into her soil to nourish the next cycle of life with the one that came before. She gives peace and compassion to the dead. Just as a rose's bud must bloom, it must also decay and return to the Goddess to help feed the next cycle so that the rose might be reborn and bloom again.

The earthly representation of the Goddess, women, and women's bodies, are literally sacred. Because Woman is of the Goddess, everything from her breasts to her vagina and even her menstrual blood embodies the Goddess's sacredness.

We have seen in this chapter that the Goddess encompasses the whole of the fertile Earth; women on this plane are representations of the Goddess. We have also looked at the different aspects of the Goddess:

- The Maiden, young and fertile aspect of the Goddess.

- The Mother, the nurturing and fertile land producing the harvests of the year.
- The Crone, mature, wise, reaping and taking back into herself the spent shells of the deceased, to nourish the next lives to come.

The God

The God has many names: Pan, Herne, Zeus, Apollo, and so on. Numerous books have been written about the God. In this section we will study the main attributes of the God as a whole without focusing on any single story or cultural depiction of him. (See the Appendix for additional reading materials on the God.) For now we will look at the cycles he exhibits and how these cycles relate to nature and our lives.

In the beginning, the oldest view of the God was the hunter and provider for the Goddess and the people. Early humans were nomadic hunter-gatherers who relied on successful hunts to survive, especially in the lean winter months when people couldn't gather plants for food. The hunt was survival. So they went to the God for help for a successful hunt.

These older Gods were usually depicted with horns, hence the Horned God of nature. Because of his fertility aspect, both for herds and humans, he is often depicted with an erect penis. An early image of the God shows a shaman dressed like the Horned God of the hunt; the image was dated around 13,000 BC. And researchers found this image as part of cave paintings in the Cave of the Trois Frères in southwestern France.

The shaman would direct ceremonial dances enacting a symbolic hunt that was successful. This would insure that the real hunt was successful, which in turn would insure that the tribe survived. These ceremonies integrated what we now call *sympathetic magic*, "magic based on the assumption that a person or thing can be supernaturally affected through its name or an object representing it" (Merriam-Webster.com).

When early humans discovered agriculture and started to grow their food instead of going out and gathering it, the God's role morphed into the vegetation god. Now he became the fertilizing force that made plants grow. He penetrates the Goddess and is reborn as the grains of the harvest. Sometimes seen as the sun, his fertilizing rays descend and make the plants grow. The Goddess was the round, ripe fruit. The God was the tall stalks of grain in the wheat field, which were cut down at harvest. The old folk song "John Barleycorn must die" illustrates this concept of the God.

As the moon represents the Goddess, the Sun symbolizes the God (think Apollo). The Sun rules the sky and sends his fertilizing rays down to Mother Earth. Unlike the moon's gentle, soothing light that nurtures our dreams and lulls us into sleep, the Sun is strong and shines his brilliant light down upon us. His light gives us thought and intelligence to manipulate the seen world.

The Goddess represents the fertile field, and the God represents the seed that penetrates the soil and fertilizes her. The God stands for the penetrating and fertilizing aspect of the All.

As the Goddess has different phases of change, so too does the God. The God's cycle changes with the turning of the seasons. Just like the Goddess, these changes follow the turning of the wheel of the year. His cycle starts at Yule during the winter solstice, when the virgin Goddess gives birth to the God. At this time of the year, the Sun's rays are weak like an infant. As the advancing year turns, the Sun God's rays become stronger, and by spring they are strong enough to create new growth. Now the animals are producing their young—another sign of his growing power.

During the spring he mates with the Goddess, which insures the summer's bounty and also insures his own rebirth at the next Yule. From spring he continues to grow in strength, and by midsummer he becomes the adult God. Midsummer represents the height of his power; this is the Earth's most bountiful time of year as well with its vegetables and fruits. As the year moves from summer to fall, he begins to wane. His rays become less potent, and he becomes the mature master.

As the seasons progress, the Sun God willingly sacrifices his life with the last harvest as it's cut down at Samhain (the Sabbat that marks the last harvest of the year). The Goddess then takes him back into her cauldron to await his rebirth at the next Yule. During this time he becomes the God of Death and rules the Summerland, or afterlife, with the dead. (By the way, you will learn more about Sabbats such as Yule and Samhain in Chapter 5.)

The Sun God has the role of the sacrificial God, for he is seen as the grains themselves. The people, understanding this, cut down the God at the last harvest, accepting his willing sacrifice of himself to feed his children. In the fall, with the harvest done and the death of the God fulfilled, his role changes, and he becomes the God of Death.

Now, as the Lord of the Underworld, he gives rest and peace to those who have gone before. He becomes Herne the Hunter, the leader of the Wild Hunt, riding through the winter's night to collect souls to take to the underworld.

Sacred Vow

As discussed above, the God and Goddess have many roles in the cycle of life and even in death. Their cycles of life reflect to us our own life's path. Through the Gods we see where we have been and where we are going. They teach us not to fear death and to honor life. We see their joy of living and the sacrifices they make for us every year. The Goddess and God love us and teach us to cherish each turning of the seasons. They reenact their sacred vow to us, which is to love each other and all of their children who live on the planet.

They enact this cycle of life for us in its entirety, over and over, year after year. From this we learn the way to immortality: the cycle of life and death through the reincarnation process. In its simplest form, reincarnation happens when a being dies and returns again by being reborn into a new body here on this physical plane.

We have seen how the God has changed over time, from hunter God to vegetation God, and how he even changes his roles during the same year. The God changes for the needs of his children through time and season, caring for us and creating abundance for us.

Chapter Questions

1. Name the different aspects of the Goddess.
2. What roles does the Goddess fulfill?
3. How do the seasons relate to the Goddess and her different aspects?
4. Name the different aspects of the God.
5. What role(s) does the God fulfill?
6. How do the seasons relate to the God and his different aspects?

CHAPTER 4:
TO BE IN A COVEN OR TO BE A SOLITARY

Deciding to participate in a coven or remain a solitary practitioner is an essential personal choice. Both options have advantages and disadvantages. You have to decide what is best for you.

Before we begin exploring these two paths, however, let me emphasize something that I said earlier in the book: You do **NOT** have to have sex with anyone to practice the Craft. If anyone tells you otherwise, they are lying. Don't listen to those who try to manipulate you into doing something you feel is wrong or uncomfortable. If any group claiming to be a coven tries to pressure you sexually, then that group is **NOT** a true coven of the Craft. The unscrupulous people who try this may call themselves Wiccans, but they are **NOT** Wiccan. They are liars who use people. So, if you become involved in a group like this, then leave it immediately.

The Coven

True covens of Wicca provide wonderful bonding and growth opportunities. Since covens are close-knit groups, you have support for personal matters. Also, when performing magick, covens can provide good training and feedback about how things went. Magick often becomes more powerful with the combined effort of many witches.

Many Wiccan coven members enjoy marvelous camaraderie with their coven mates. If you decide to be in a coven, you will most likely get together to celebrate Sabbats and Esbats together, which can be very rewarding experiences. Being in a coven gives you the opportunity to discuss and ask questions about Witchcraft. Most importantly, you will get answers to your questions. This is indeed a great learning tool to have.

But covens are not always sunshine. People have quarrels. And getting everyone together at the same place and at the same time can be tricky. It can feel like herding cats.

Finding the right coven can be the biggest challenge. You must educate yourself on the various traditions and types of covens so that you can choose the one that is best for you. For example, some covens, particularly in British Traditional Wicca, practice skyclad or ritual nudity. If this makes you uncomfortable, then that's not the type of coven for you.

Even those covens in the same tradition can be quite unique unto themselves. Although they may practice the same way, the different personalities in each coven differentiate how each group is run. You need to find the right fit for you.

The Solitary Path

Being a solitary practitioner eliminates the need to be at a specific place at a specific time. There are no quarrels with others about the format of ritual or the ways to do things. You can do ritual when, how, and where you want. For many people, this is a big plus! No one tells you what to do or how to do it. No one forgets to bring something to a gathering. It's just you and the Gods.

Some Wiccans seek to augment their knowledge with online resources. Sometimes, that can be helpful. However, *each person must be careful* because one does not know who is actually posting such material. Also, it has been demonstrated time and again that one mistake or false idea can be promulgated throughout the Internet.

But being a solitary practitioner has its downsides as well. It can be lonely work. You don't get feedback with your workings. Finding a reliable and knowledgeable person to answer your questions can be daunting. You will not have a group to consult when you get stuck in your practice. You'll also miss out on the celebratory joy of the Sabbats.

Whichever path you take is your personal choice. Each is valid. I suggest trying both to see which one you prefer.

Chapter Questions

1. What do you call a Wiccan who practices his or her Craft alone?
2. Why is requiring sex wrong to the Craft?
3. What is a coven?

CHAPTER 5:
SABBATS AND ESBATS

The Sabbats

The Sabbats are the best moments of the year. They are times of celebration! Can you say party? In Sabbats, Wiccans celebrate the cycles of the seasons and how the God and Goddess change during each cycle throughout the year. Family and friends complete these special times.

Generally, Wiccans do not practice magickal "work" on Sabbats. Instead, Sabbats are celebratory times when friends and family gather and honor the Gods.

Wiccans typically celebrate eight Sabbats each year:

o **Imbolc**, around February 2

o **Ostara**, around March 22, Spring (Vernal) Equinox

o **Beltane**, on May 1

o **Litha** (Midsummer), around June 22, Summer Solstice

o **Lammas** (Lughnasadh), on August 1

o **Mabon**, around September 22, Autumn Equinox

o **Samhain**, on October 31-November1

o **Yule**, around December 22, Winter Solstice

The Sabbats break down as follows:

- The High Sabbats: Samhain, Imbolc, Beltane, Lammas. (The High Sabbats are called the Cross-Quarter days, so-called because they are mid-way between the solstices and equinoxes which form a cross on the wheel of the year.)
- The Low Sabbats are the Equinoxes and Solstices: Ostara, Litha, Mabon, and Yule

The Wheel of the Year, illustrated in the photograph above, shows the cycle of the Wiccan annual festivals or Sabbats. Each Sabbat celebrates a different cycle of life and death, and each shows the changing seasons heading toward harvest times to the time of rebirth and growth.

The Wheel of the Year takes us on the journey of the life cycle—both for the Gods and ourselves. We see the God's birth at Yule, watch him grow with the seasons and sexually mature at Ostara. At Midsummer, we see him at the height of his glory. We watch him wane until his sacrificial death at Samhain.

The Wheel of the Year also shows the cycles of the Goddess. She becomes young once more as the Maiden aspect at Imbolc, turning into the Mother at Midsummer, becoming the Crone at Samhain, only to turn back to her youthful self at Yule.

Yule

At Yule the God's rebirth from the virgin Goddess is celebrated. Some Christians might say, "Wait. Virgin is an important word to us."

Here's the real story. "Virgin birth" is actually pre-Christian, and it was a pagan idea originally. How? Thousands of years ago, before people kept animals and figured out that female sheep do not get pregnant if a male is kept away from them, people thought only women were able to make new life and that was magical. Cause and effect was hard to see when it was nine months between the act of sex and birth. So it appeared that all women gave birth without men. A number of Wiccan scholars suggest that the original meaning of *virgin* means pure, unadulterated, nothing added, and no men in the process. The first idea that men were involved was when Isis had sex with the dead Osiris to give birth to Horus, documented in Temple wall paintings in Ancient Egypt. This was after the Egyptians began herding cattle, goats, sheep and pigs.

Finally, having sex with "the God" was very common in the Greek and Roman pagan religions, with Zeus having sex with women to produce Hercules, Helen of Troy, and even Alexander the Great.

Let's continue with the Goddess at Yule time. The Goddess turns once more into her youthful form, as the young virgin mother. At Yule the Goddess is the new mother with the God as her new child.

Yule is also known as the Winter Solstice, the longest night of the year. During early human history, people feared that the sun would not reappear without help. With this belief began the custom of lighting candles and fires to lure back the sun. It was believed that this ritual would help the God to be reborn (as the solar deity) from the Goddess by helping the Goddess to have an easy delivery.

Evergreen trees are associated with the Yule season. Our ancestors revered evergreens. Why? Beginning with the Celtic Druids of central Europe during the Late Bronze Age, evergreens became sacred due to their representation of everlasting life. They saw that evergreen trees were the one source of life that continued to live and stay green throughout the year—even in the deepest winter. These trees didn't die with the rest of the plants during the cold months.

The people of the day brought evergreens into their homes and decorated them with small gifts to the God and Goddess. Candles were placed on the bows of the trees (I do *not* recommend this due to fire hazard). Yule trees were born, which is where Christians got their Christmas tree. The Yule tree was so popular that the Christian Church couldn't stamp out the practice. Pagans 1, Church 0. And the rest is history.

For Wiccans, Yule logs are another nice custom. The pagans of northern Europe began the custom of cutting off a piece of a Yule tree (usually an evergreen oak tree, also called a live oak) to save for a ritual the following year. For the ritual, people would gather on a hillside for a sacred bonfire and celebration. Afterward, they brought home a lit branch from the bonfire to light their fires at home, which had all been extinguished prior to the sacred gathering. They would then light their last year's Yule log in their fireplace to bless their home. This tradition is still carried on today.

At modern Yule celebrations, we gather with our loved ones to enjoy the merriment of the Sabbat with food and drink. We open gifts and sing songs about the God's return. Even those without fireplaces can get commercially made Yule logs with candleholders.

Imbolc
Midway between the Winter Solstice and the Spring Equinox, you will find Imbolc, which is celebrated on

February 2nd. This time of year the light is beginning to return to the world. Like the Yule Sabbat, the Imbolc Sabbat is also associated with fire. Can you see a theme here? What's the reason for this? Fire honors the God and gives him strength. And who doesn't like a nice warm fire on a chilly night during the cold part of the year?

At Imbolc the Goddess has finally recovered from the strains of giving birth to the God. Ready to start the new growing season of the year, the Goddess becomes the young maiden once more. The act of purification encompasses a large part of this Sabbat.

At Imbolc we honor the Goddess Bridget, one of the Goddesses of fertility and birth. The Celtic Goddess Bridget rules fire and the art of forge craft or metalsmithing. Bridget provides inspiration and represents domestic arts like healing and cooking. We often use fires in the home as a nice way to honor Bridget, the Goddess of the Earth.

Wiccans memorialize Imbolc, the time of purification, with the tradition of lighting candles. Candles provide inspiration and symbolize the growing light and strength from the Sun God. Candles help coax the light to come into the year and bring on the bounty of nature.

There is a bit of a controversy about the definition of the term Imbolc. Back in 1988, authors Janet and Stewart Farrar translated Imbolc as "in the belly." This refers to the coming of new life to the land. However, many Wiccans prefer to tie the term to the Old Irish word *oimelc*, which is ewe's milk. After all, it is at this time of the year that the ewes give birth to their lambs. Since the ewes' lactation period peaks at Imbolc, Wiccans view milk as an appropriate drink for this Sabbat. They enjoy lamb's meat cooked on a sacred fire, paying homage to the Goddess. (See Appendix B for a lamb stew recipe.)

As a mark of beginnings (births and the starting of new life), Imbolc is a good time for initiations, purification, and rededications. This Sabbat coincides with the waxing of the year, when our intentions can grow along with the light. And so our dedications to the Gods grow in strength at this time.

Ostara

Ostara happens at the Spring (Vernal) Equinox. The length of the day becomes equal to that of the night, and the light finally overcomes the darkness of winter. Ostara's theme is fertility. The God courts the Goddess, and their sexual energies of desire flow over the Earth, leading to a burst of new life and growth upon the land by the plants and the animals. Here the God and Goddess's desire to mate drives the Earth and its inhabitants to also mate and bring new life to the land.

The Teutonic Goddess of spring, Easter, brings her symbol of the egg and her patron animal, the rabbit. Wiccans celebrate Easter during the Ostara Sabbat. The Christian Church tried to stamp out celebrations of Easter and her symbols of fertility (the egg and the rabbit), but they had become too deeply embedded in the people's hearts. Christians got their Easter eggs and rabbits from this Goddess. How many Christians know that when they celebrate Easter, they're using a term originated by Pagans?

Generally, eggs are a popular representation of fertility and new life. Early Wiccans revered the "cosmic egg" for the secrets it held. It looked like a stone, but it held life within, and life came forth from it.

Wiccan activities on Ostara include coloring eggs and decorating them with fertility symbols, then hiding them for children to find.

Beltane

On May 1st, Beltane celebrates the beginning of summer. Bale or "bon" fires are an important part of the Beltane Sabbat. In the Beltane celebrations of old, all fires at home or in shops were extinguished and then re-lit from the sacred bonfires that blazed on the tops of the surrounding hills. This was also the time when the herds were blessed by having cattle marched between bonfires. (This is how fire and purification are connected.) Such a process was thought to bring good luck and fertility and to protect the cattle during the year.

The Sabbat Beltane coincides with the period of time when the God actually impregnates the Goddess. This sacred act insures the continued fertility for crops and animals throughout the light half of the year (between the Spring and Fall Equinoxes.) A popular symbol for this sacred act is the May Pole, which represents the impregnation of the Goddess. A May Pole is a pole set erect in the ground with ribbons attached on the top. People then each take a ribbon and dance in a weaving pattern around the pole. The pole represents the God's phallus, and the colorful ribbons that the dancers wind around the May Pole represent the Goddess with her flowers a-blooming. And so the impregnation of the Goddess is fulfilled.

As Beltane celebrates the beginning of summer, many Wiccans celebrate more time in the sun. For me, lemons, yellow in color, represent the sun. Lemons are a great way to enjoy the summer since they're refreshing in lemonade and other dishes. In appendix B I give you my famous Lemon Bar recipe.

(See Appendix B for a great Lemon Bars recipe.)

Litha

The Summer Solstice, Litha, also known as Midsummer, represents when the God is at the height of his power and fertility. The sun now takes its longest path across the sky, and we experience the longest day of the year. This completes the sun's waxing cycle and marks the beginning of the waning part of the solar year. The days become increasingly shorter until the Wheel of the Year returns to Yule when the days once again wax with the sun.

Wiccans enjoy collecting and drying herbs during Litha. Many take nice walks out in nature to harvest these herbs. Herbs harvested during this period have greater magickal powers than herbs gathered at other times of the year. Herbs reach their peak of strength and potency during Litha.

Once again, the bonfire holds a prominent place. The God rises to his peak as his power and strength expand at Litha.

Not all covens have access to open places that permit bonfires, but that doesn't mean these groups can't celebrate the summer Sabbats. They just need to develop their own symbolic representations. For example, when my coven meets for Litha, we do a barbeque. Meat and fire form a good combo for this Sabbat! Yum!

Lammas

On August 1st, Lammas, also called Lughnasadh (the Celtic first day of autumn), starts the first of the three Wiccan harvest festivals. Known as the time when the God starts to wane in his power, Lammas, or "loaf-mass," celebrates the first grains harvested that season. During the Lammas Sabbat, Wiccans offer up the first sheaf of the harvest to the God and Goddess to thank them for their blessing of the harvest yield.

Wiccans love to feast, and this is the best time of year to do it! Since grains are a prominent part of the Lammas Sabbat, we celebrate by making breads and other baked goods from the first wheat or corn produced. The different breads, beers, and other foods produced and consumed at this time remind us of the bounty that the Gods have given us. (See Appendix B for a kickin' Pumpkin Bread recipe.)

Mabon

The year's second balance between light and dark we call Mabon. Many know it as the Autumn Equinox, when the days continue to grow shorter and the dark begins to take over the light. With longer nights and fewer daylight hours, we observe the continued waning power of the God.

As the second of the three harvest festivals, Mabon (also known as the witches' thanksgiving) offers us the opportunity to give thanks to the God and Goddess for all the bounty and sacrifices they have made for us during the year. During Mabon, friends and family come together for a meal of thanksgiving. This is another feasting time. The feast includes bread, corn, squash, autumn vegetables, and—lest you forget—wine, beer, and mead are all part of the banquet!

We give thanks to the God and Goddess for all they have given us at Mabon, both the mundane and the magickal. At Mabon I have one ritual to honor the Gods in which I pour some wine onto the ground as a sacrifice. This small ritual represents the intention of observing that the God remains alive until Samhain when he sacrifices himself so that humanity may live.

Samhain

The final harvest Sabbat, Samhain, corresponds with the period of the year when the last crops are gathered and put into storage for the cold winter months. Samhain arrives at the time that the Western World calls Halloween.

The God makes his ultimate sacrifice during Samhain. But fear not! His sacrifice is made willingly. He does it for his children. The God's sacrifice is represented by the final harvest being cut down so that we may have food to last through the winter. As mentioned before, the song "John Barleycorn" illustrates this sacrifice.

In the past, at this time of the year, the cattle and pigs were culled. Only those that were strong enough to live through the harsh winter months were kept alive. The meat of the livestock was salted and cured to provide sustenance to the people during the long winter.

Samhain is also known as the witches' New Year, an idea that came from the Celts. The Celts understood that this time started the beginning of the year. Why? Because they believed a person's new life actually started at death. Most Wiccans believe in reincarnation. This belief coincides with the fact that one must die in order to be reborn into a new life. This is what the God does when he sacrifices his life. He resides in the underworld to await rebirth at Yule.

After turning to the Samhain Sabbat, which represents death, the Wheel of the Year continues turning toward Yule, the beginning, representing life and rebirth. The eternal cycle of reincarnation is celebrated during Samhain. The old God dies to be reborn again at Yule.

At Samhain, we honor and communicate with the dead. This is when the Veil between the worlds becomes its thinnest. The Veil is the doorway or curtain that separates the land of the living and the land of the dead. A modern approximation to Samhain would be Mexico's Day of the Dead.

Samhain remains my favorite holiday. It honors what Western society is frightened of and makes it something beautiful. We honor the dead, we don't fear them. And I don't mind dressing up either!

Some of my few good childhood memories include decorating our front yard as a little haunted house. I feel that my lifelong attraction to this holiday is about looking beyond this life to the spiritual realm, and being at peace with it.

The Esbats

Esbats, Wiccan meetings we hold once a month during the full moon, are where we come together to perform magick and talk to the God and Goddess.

The Esbats I have attended have helped me to grow by leaps and bounds. It was through my coven's Esbats that I learned to meditate effectively, which has become an important part of my inner work. During the Esbats, meditation has made me a stronger individual and has brought me closer to the Gods as well as to myself.

As previously mentioned, I used to have image issues. I hated my body and myself. But I found truth through meditation. I learned that the Goddess takes many forms and that each is perfect in its own right. I learned that I was made in the Goddess's image and that my body is her body. I learned that I am perfect just as I am. Therefore, I can no more call myself "thunder thighs" than I can the Goddess herself. Because of the Gods and these meditations during the Esbats, I have become more confident than I have ever been before. I now strive to serve others and to let them know the Gods' message for them.

Esbats are times for the coven's magickal workings. These workings help us focus on growth and self-improvement. We use the phases of the moon as a guide to determine what kind of spells we do. The moon's many phases are important because of the different energies they produce during each cycle throughout the year.

Let's say you want to do a spell of increase, such as a money spell that would increase your income. For the best results, you would conduct the spell during the waxing (increase) or full moon. Aim to work the spell during the full moon; Wiccans know this time of increase is auspicious.

Perhaps, you want to work a spell of decrease to lose weight. Do it on a waning moon (on its way toward decreasing).

Warning: Do NOT do magick on the fully dark moon, otherwise known as a new moon. *Only* Advanced Wiccans with great knowledge should work at this time.

Each full moon has a name that corresponds to its month. Each name describes the time of the year that it occurs. The names of the moons are:

January	Wolf Moon
February	Chaste Moon
March	Seed Moon
April	Hare Moon / Thunder Moon
May	Dyad Moon
June	Mead Moon / Honey Moon
July	Wort Moon
August	Barley Moon
September	Wine Moon
October	Blood Moon / Harvest Moon
November	Oak Moon / Hunter Moon
December	Snow Moon

The 13th moon of the year is the Witches Moon

Conclusion

We have taken a tour through the different Sabbats. We have learned how each Sabbat fits together to make a complete life cycle for the Gods and us—from the blessed birth of the Sun God at Yule to enjoying the youthful play of the Gods at Ostara. We have seen the mating cycle of the God and Goddess at Beltane in May, the glory of summer, and how the Gods bestow their bounty on us, as well as the God's sacrificial death at Samhain. We've also explored the full moons and the Esbats where we honor the God and Goddess.

Chapter Questions

1. Which are the High Sabbats?
2. Which are the Minor/Lesser Sabbats?
3. When is the beginning of the New Year for Wiccans?

CHAPTER 6
THE ELEMENTS

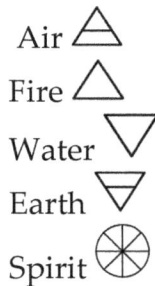

Air △
Fire △
Water ▽
Earth ▽
Spirit ✹

In most Eastern and pre-Christian Celtic religions, the building blocks for all things are the five elements: Air, Fire, Water, Earth, and Spirit. Life can't survive without each of these. We all need warmth (Fire), a place to call our own (Earth), air to breathe, and water to drink. Everything in the physical world is made up of at least one element, but most often it is a combination of two or more. We need all five to be completely balanced.

The pentacle represents life with each point indicating one of the four elements and a fifth for Spirit. Soon, we will talk about each element's Elemental, a spirit or being that is completely made of that element. We can understand the world we live in by studying the elements and how they interact in our environment and our spiritual lives.

A note on the elements: The feminine elements are seen as receptive, that is, you put things into water and earth. On the other hand masculine elements are seen as active. Air and fire move themselves and transform other things.

Air

Air represents the direction East.

The sun rises in the East. Associated with the time of dawn, air belongs during the morning. East means new beginnings. So anything that begins or "dawns" is of the Air symbol. Air represents thought, and new ideas dawn in our heads all the time. East is a male element. This is not to say that females don't have the Air element in them. But Air is considered to be a masculine element. (Remember "animus" and "anima" in Chapter 3.)

Air reflects thought and intelligence. Simply put, Air is pure thought. We use the attributes of Air to figure out our problems. The skill of problem solving is Air's strength. Think of math and science as subjects ruled by Air.

Things that represent Air are feathers/birds of all kinds, clouds, dust devils, wind chimes, and incense smoke to name a few.

The sylph is the Elemental of Air. Some artists have depicted sylphs as human figures with wings. Sylphs are often seen in cloud formations. Note that an Elemental is an entity that embodies one specific element.

In many Tarot decks, swords represent Air. Since Air is the element of thought and intellect, Tarot swords represent ideas and other qualities of Air. But just like a real sword, thoughts can cut two ways. They can be freeing or debilitating, just as having a life-altering epiphany is to having depression.

Fire

Fire represents the direction South.

Fire is associated with noon, the hottest time of the day. As with Air, Fire is seen as a male/masculine element. Fire is action! Fire represents your will. It is the spark that sets you into motion. It is the energy that moves you to finish your housework. Fire is represented by embers, the sun, hot chili peppers, and a flame from a candle.

Salamanders are the Elemental spirits of Fire. The Fire salamander is seen as dragon-like. Like flames, they are shape-shifters. They are sometimes depicted with wings and human faces, much like sylphs.

In many Tarot decks, wands represent Fire. Whereas Air is the beginning or the plan you start with, Fire sets that plan into action!

Fire also transforms. It changes whatever it touches, consuming it and converting it into something new. The Phoenix is a good example of this. It is consumed by fire and then rises from its own ashes as something new. In a sense, it is being reborn out of its own destruction.

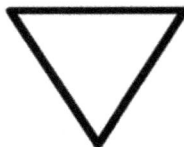

$$\triangledown$$

Water

Water represents the direction West.

Water's corresponding time of day is at sunset. Water is associated with the moon and with birth, death, and rebirth. It also has to do with feelings and emotions. Water connotes strong feelings such as love, desire, hate, joy, and sorrow. Water is seen as a feminine element. Things that represent water are seashells, seaweed, water, sponges, and fish.

Because of its association with death, Water is also associated with the Summerlands (afterlife). Many folkloric traditions include a journey over a body of water to reach their afterlife.

The Undine is the Elemental spirit in water. Undines are water entities that can manifest themselves in many forms, from mermaids to the sirens of the sea.

In many Tarot decks, cups represent Water. In Tarot, cups represent emotions. Cups are also associated with birth, death, and rebirth.

You may recall that my name is Moonwater SilverClaw. I chose this name because I feel connected to water. My mother still tells tales of how, as a child, I'd find any puddle in a two-mile radius. To this day I enjoy the water whether I'm snorkeling or doing undersea helmet diving.

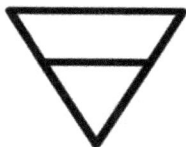

Earth

Earth represents the direction North.

Midnight is the time that is associated with this element. Earth stands for stability, foundations, and commitment. The greatest image of Earth is Mother Earth or Gaia herself. Earth is seen as a feminine element. Earth is also stillness. Earth is represented by rocks, crystals, dirt, and fossils.

Gnomes are the Elemental spirits of Earth. Gnomes are strong and squat. Their skin is the colors of the Earth with its many shades of brown to black.

In many Tarot decks, Earth is represented by coins or pentacles. Coins in the Tarot connote physical labors and the fruits of those labors. They often refer to physical possessions, such as money, cars, and houses.

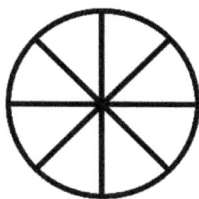

Spirit

The fifth element is Spirit.

The fifth element does not have a specific direction or a specific time in our twenty-four-hour day. That being said, Spirit is what creates the life within us. It is literally the divine spark that we all need to be alive. There is no Elemental associated with Spirit.

What we call the "soul" is in fact a piece of the God and Goddess, or "The All." Every one of us has this element within us. It is the element that makes all living things divine.

In Conclusion

We have seen how each element fits into the whole—a whole being. The whole completes the balance of life. Each element has a role in our lives. And in its own unique way, each element contributes to create and sustain life. They help us live more fulfilling lives every day.

Chapter Questions

1. Name the Elements and the direction associated with each one.
2. Match the times of day with their elements.
3. Death is represented by which direction?

CHAPTER 7:
THE TOOLS

Wiccans use many different tools to practice the Craft. Some of these tools may be familiar to you, while others may not be as recognizable. Each tool has a different function. The following section lists some common tools and explains how they are used.

A note on secondhand items: Don't pick out tools that merely look cool. They have to feel right to you, too. If you find a tool that somehow doesn't feel right to you, it is not the right one. Put it back.

Trust me on this. Years ago, I would go into thrift shops to find some implements. One day, I reached for a particular glass, and suddenly I had a bitter taste in my mouth. That was weird! That was some bad energy! I put it down quickly and moved on.

When you encounter a secondhand item, you don't know what energy it has if was pre-owned. Just be careful and use your intuition.

Also, be sure to do a cleansing and dedication ritual before using a new tool. The Casting Circle Chapter provides you with a simple dedication ritual you might use.

• **Athame:** The athame is a ritual dagger, usually double edged with a black handle. The athame is used to consecrate (sanctify) the other elements, such as the salt and water on an altar, and to focus and channel energy. Since it is never used to cut material objects, its blade need not be sharp. The athame is used only to cut energy. The athame is considered a male or phallic symbol.

• **Bell or Chime:** The bell represents the female aspect. When rung, its sound creates a positive energy wave that drives away unwanted entities. It is usually used at the beginning of the ritual to cleanse the space. The bell also can be used as a timing device to signal the next phase of a ritual, for instance, to summon a person into the circle.

• **Besom:** The besom or broom is seen as the sexual union of the God and Goddess. The handle is considered the phallic male symbol that penetrates the bundle of twigs, which is representative of the female vagina. It is used at handfastings (weddings) to not only symbolize fertility but also to exemplify crossing the threshold into a new life together. The besom is also used to clean or sweep away negative energy. You need not actually sweep up dirt to do this; the besom sweeps the negative energies away from a space.

- **Boline:** Unlike the athame, the boline knife has a white handle and is used to actually cut physical things. The boline is sometimes used to scribe letters and symbols on candles for magick work. It is the blade used for physical work.

- **Candles:** Wiccans use candles in many ways. Candles are used to cast spells, to provide lighting, to indicate the Quarters/directions in a cast circle, and to represent the God and Goddess on the altar.

- **Censer:** There are different kinds of censers (vessels). Depending on the type of incense you use, some hold burning charcoals for raw incense. Others hold cones or sticks of incense, depending on your preference.

- **Cauldron:** Cauldrons come in all shapes and sizes. They are used for making potions as well as for burning incense. Note: Be careful that the cauldron is food-safe since many are made with lead.

- **Cords:** Cords are used to do magick. Some covens use cords to indicate what degree or standing a witch has achieved in his or her coven. Each practitioner has his/her own cords that are worn around the waist.

- **Cup or Chalice:** The cup is a symbol of the womb and is thus a female symbol. It is used to hold sacred wine. During the symbolic Great Rite, an athame is dipped into a chalice filled with wine, blessing it. This act symbolizes the union of the God and Goddess. The wine is then shared among coven members after a portion of the liquid is given to the Gods as an offering.

• **Incense:** When burned, incense is used to purify or charge people and items with energy. It is seen as a male element. Different incense is used for different reasons. One use might be for drawing money toward you.

• **Offering Dishes:** These dishes are used during rituals to set aside offerings to the God and Goddess. They can be made of any material. The choice of design adds a bit of personality to an altar.

• **Pentacle:** The pentacle is a five-pointed star. Each point represents one of the elements (Fire, Water, Air, Earth, and Spirit.) Each element is needed to create life. The pentacle is used to consecrate and or bless material items. It is used as a focal point on an altar.

• **Salt:** Salt is a cleansing element. Since it represents the Earth, salt is seen as feminine. Salt is blessed and placed into water to create consecrated water, which is used to cleanse people, the circle, and the objects used in ritual.

• **Sword:** The sword is generally used to cast the sacred circle. However, if you're in a small room, you can use the athame or a wand. In this way, you avoid accidentally breaking something or hurting someone while using such a large tool. The sword, like the athame, is phallic and therefore a male symbol.

• **Wand:** Like the athame, the wand is used for directing energy. The difference is that the wand is a gentler approach to energy work. You command with an athame, but you invite with a wand. Wands can be used to cast a circle that is semi-permeable.

• **Water:** Water is used in combination with salt. Wiccans use salt to consecrate and purify the water. The salt and water mixture recreates the ocean waters and simulates the salinity of the womb. Water is seen as a feminine element.

Now I'll share a few more words on the Pentacle.

The Pentacle

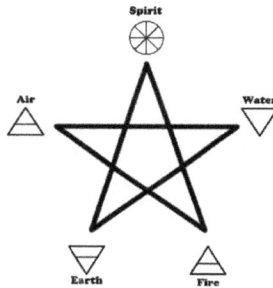

To me, the pentacle inspires feelings of warmth, awe, and joy. It stands for life—the mystery and the balance. The pentacle serves as the universal symbol of the Craft. You can find it in all occult shops and most New Age stores. Wiccans often wear a pentacle as a pendant on a necklace or a symbol on a ring. But what is this symbol, and what is the message it really conveys?

As a five-pointed star, the pentacle represents each element with one of its points. Many people have heard of the elements of Air, Fire, Water, and Earth, but they may be unfamiliar with the fifth element, Spirit. Nevertheless, all five items are needed and unique.

Air is associated with thought. Thoughts move in and out of our minds just like a light breeze flows through our hair. Thoughts are the beginning of actions; likewise, dawn represents the beginning of new things. Wiccans thereby associate Air with dawn. Further, Air relates to the direction East, where the sun comes up and begins the day.

Fire is associated with action. Besides keeping us warm, it is the spark that gets us into motion. It motivates our will producing results on the physical plane. Fire is also associated with the direction South. Our ancestors (from Europe) understood that going towards the South, the lands were warmer.

Water is associated with emotion, which flows through us. Every thought creates feelings. We remember grandma's cooking and get that warm fuzzy feeling inside, or we remember that fight with our partner that made us so mad! Water is associated with the West, which is associated with crossing the River Styx and going to the land of the dead.

Earth is associated with stability and with its function as the foundation for other things. Earth keeps us stable and often represents the many mundane things that we need in life. Earth represents the physicality of our bodies and the ground we stand upon. Earth's direction is North, and it is represented by mountains, rocks, and crystals.

Spirit is the unique element that ties the rest together. It is our spirit that the Gods have given us, which makes us alive. You cannot have life without the other four. We need air to breathe, fire to keep us warm, and water to drink. We need the physicality of our bodies (represented as Earth) to interact with our surroundings. But we cannot truly be us without spirit. What is a soul? It is a piece of the Gods that they place within all that is alive. This soul animates our Air, Fire, Water, and Earth into a living being.

Spirit is a crucial element that is too often overlooked. Spirit is the miracle of life itself. We are the pentacle. We are life.

In Conclusion

This chapter gave us a brief look at the main tools used in the Craft. From the athame to water to the chalice, we have examined their roles and discussed how each is used in the Craft. Next we will look at how to arrange an altar.

Chapter Questions

1. What do you use salt for?
2. What tool do you use in most cases to cast a circle?
3. What are some ways you use candles in circle?

CHAPTER 8:
YOUR ALTAR

When I first started learning about altar setups, it took me a long time to remember where everything should be placed. I felt self conscious about making mistakes. My mentor would simply smile at me and move the item I had misplaced to where it should reside on the altar.

My point is: do *not* beat yourself up if you get it wrong. Use the picture provided here for as long as you need it. Note that there are many ways to set up an altar, and each person or group has a specific method. This chapter shows you an example of a typical altar setup.

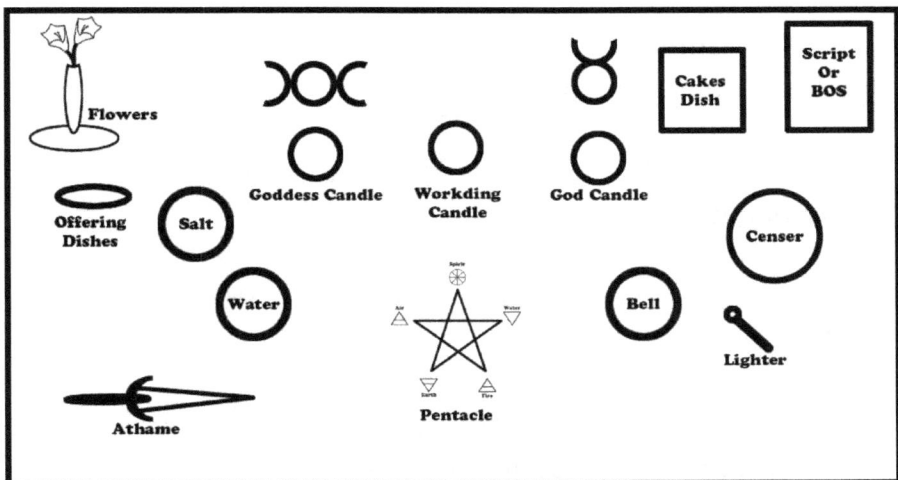

What's on an altar? Let's start with the upper right side of the table and move around clockwise.

1) **Cakes/Bread:** It is acceptable to use bread, cupcakes, cookies, or even a power bar. It should contain carbohydrates to nourish the body and replenish the energy you use during the ritual.

2) **Censer & Incense:** In this case, the incense burner holds cone incense. However, it is acceptable to burn any kind of incense you choose. Remember that incense, when burned, represents Air on your altar.

3) **Taper:** The taper is for lighting candles. You begin by using a lighter to ignite the wick of the working candle. Then, you bring the taper to the working candle and ignite the wick of the taper. Now with the lit taper you ignite the other candles on your altar.

4) **Lighter:** The lighter is used to light the working candle. Any type of lighter may be used.

5) **Bell/Chime**: A bell or chime is needed for different purposes during a ritual.

6) **Pentacle:** The pentacle is used to help focus your attention on your goal.

7) **Athame:** The athame knife is used to direct power and can cast circles.

8) **Bowl with Water:** Water is one of the five elements. It is used together with salt to make consecrated water.

9) **Dish with Salt:** Salt represents the Earth. It is placed into water to make consecrated water.

10) **Chalice with Wine:** As you remember, the cup is a female symbol. In a ritual, the cup holds the wine or juice that is to be blessed. (It is acceptable to use juice instead of wine if you do not drink alcohol.)

11) **Offering Dishes:** These dishes are used to "offer up," as an offering, part of your blessed food from your "cakes and wine" ceremony. We will discuss that later. You can also offer up flowers, which pay tribute to nature and the Goddess.

12) **Goddess Candle & God Candle:** These are the candles that represent the God and Goddess.

13) **Working Candle:** The working candle is positioned between the God and Goddess candle. Use this candle to light the other candles during a ritual. The working candle represents the element Fire on your altar.

You will find that, with a little practice, setting up your altar will become second nature to you.

Notice that I do not include cords. This is because Wiccans that practice outside of a coven are unlikely to use this tool. The besom, or broom, is another tool that is not always used. And, of course, it's hard to fit a sword on the altar!

The basic setup listed here will get you started doing rituals. The Casting Circle Chapter will teach you how these tools work together. The tools need not cost you a lot of money. I found many of my tools in secondhand stores. You can also use antiques or the latest designs from your local artists. The choice is yours.

As mentioned previously, however, you must be wary of secondhand items that may contain negative energy. Pick out tools that feel right to you. If one doesn't feel right, then don't use it. Always do a cleansing and dedication ritual before using any new tool.

In Conclusion

This chapter has revealed the items needed for your altar. As I mentioned, with practice, you'll be able to set up your altar with ease.

Chapter Questions

1. Name the candles used on your altar.
2. Name three tools and their related elements.
3. What is the athame knife used for?

CHAPTER 9:

MEDITATION

Meditation is a key aspect of the Wiccan practice. The practice of meditation helps us stay balanced, calm, and happy. In addition, meditation helps us to communicate with the Gods. Meditation is used as a teaching tool, from gaining self-awareness in a coven setting to a relaxation technique that enriches mental health. Through meditation, a Wiccan talks to his or her spirit guides and communes with the God and Goddess.

A note about spirit guides: These are beings who are on the astral plane who assist the person to solve problems. These beings also provide essential teachings and insight.

I remember an early meditation session when I first met the Gods. On the deck of my house, I practiced a simple form of breath meditation. I focused on my breath, bringing in the loving pure energy of the universe with each inhale.

As I breathed out, I exhaled the negative stress energy from within me. I envisioned the negative energy as black smoke being released from my body. I took in the light and exhaled the black smoke.

My mind wandered, and I began speculating about the God and Goddess. This was before I really knew the Gods on a personal level. I wondered what they were really like. Who were They?

As my thoughts meandered, something happened. I became aware of two loving energies sitting next to me. The God was on my left, and the Goddess was on my right! I felt them each place a hand in my hand. They then sat quietly with me, sending me their loving energy and expressing their love for me. They expressed that I was perfect the way that I was, and that They loved me no matter what.

I couldn't see them, but I could feel them touching my hands, holding them with compassion. I felt their complete love and acceptance. I felt their warm, soft, and deep caring for my wellbeing. It was like being in a blanket of pure love. I wanted to stay like that forever. But I couldn't, and after a few minutes it was over. I will never forget that moment. I think They wanted me to know that the path I had begun with Wicca was exactly where I needed to be. And They wanted me to know that They loved me.

Let's do an exercise.

This meditation exercise is great for cleaning out the energy cobwebs in you. I can't guarantee that you will meet the Gods on this journey, but it will make you feel relaxed and calm. Try not to expect too much at first. Meditation takes practice. And don't worry if your mind wanders. Just work on pulling your mind back to the task.

Before you start, make sure you can be alone for at least

30 to 45 minutes. The more you practice, the less time you will need, although you will probably enjoy this state and wish to linger there. Turn off your cell phone, computer, and anything else that might cause a disturbance. Go into a room where you will not be disturbed.

Find a comfortable chair or, if you prefer, sit on meditation pillows. It's best not to lie down because you will probably fall asleep. Sit up so that your spine is straight. Consider reading aloud and recording the following visualization, and then replay it during your meditation session.

A Note on Chakras: The concept of chakras comes from Eastern philosophy. They are energy centers located along your spine and up through the top of your head. The first chakra, called the Root Chakra, is located at the base of your spine. Its color is red. Then there is the Sacral Chakra, and its color is orange. Continuing up, we have the Solar Plexus Chakra (yellow), the Heart Chakra (green), the Throat Chakra (blue), and the Third Eye or Brow Chakra (indigo), and finally the Crown Chakra (purple).

We move energy up through the body passing these points of power to center ourselves and to remove the energy blockages that we have. These blockages can cause disease and pain. This is the basis for energy healing.

Let's begin the meditation.

The Tree of Life Meditation
Meditation Exercise — "The Tree of Life"
Slowly breathe in and out. Breathe in the energy of love and peace (envision this as white energy). Breathe out all stress and negativity (envision this as black smoke). Keep taking deep breaths in and out. Concentrate on the white energy being breathed in and filling up your body with

loving energy. Then let go and breathe out the negative energy you see as black smoke.

As you do this, release the stresses of the day. Repeat this breathing cycle at least three times until you are comfortable and relaxed.

As your body and mind begin to relax, continue deep breathing and focus on this image:

Envision roots made up of energy sprout from the bottoms of your feet. With each breath, extend the roots farther and farther down toward Mother Earth.

Extend them down through the floor, down past the plumbing of the house, and down, down deep into Mother Earth's body. Go down to her core, to the center of her heart.

Once there, with each breath in, pull up the energy from Mother Earth. Breathe out the stress, and breathe in the blue-green energy of the Mother.

Pull the energy up through your roots, up past the plumbing of the house, past the floor, and into your feet. The energy feels clean and refreshing.

Breathe in deeply. Pull the blue-green energy up into your legs and past your knees. Pull it up, up into your Root Chakra at the base of your spine. Let it fill your body, going up, up into your Sacral Chakra and continuing to your Solar Plexus Chakra. Breathing in deeply, draw the energy up, up into your Heart Chakra. Let the energy flow down your arms and into your hands. Feel your body relax as the energy fills it.

Breathing in, draw the energy up into your Throat Chakra.

Concentrate on the blue-green energy filling your body. When you are ready, with another breath in, breathe the energy up into your Third Eye Chakra.

Using your breath, draw the energy up into your Crown Chakra. Feel the energy flow throughout your body.

With another breath in, pull the energy up and out of your head. The energy forms like branches toward the Sky above you. Continue and let the branches flow up to the universe and out into the cosmos.

Draw down the golden energy of the Sky and universe into you. Continue to let the Sky energy intermingle and mix with the Earth energy that is already there. Pull it down through your body and into your arms.

Continue breathing deeply, mixing and pulling the energies down to your Heart Chakra.

Breathe in again, pulling the energy of the universe down into your Solar Plexus Chakra.

Continue pulling in the energy. Let it flow into you. Pull it into your Root Chakra. Breathing deeply, pull it down your legs and down to your feet.

Feel the energy from both the Earth Mother and the Sky Father that is within you. Enjoy this relaxing and cleansing energy.

In a moment or two, slowly start to pull your branches back within you, pulling them in with each breath.

Let any extra energy dissipate through the roots that you had placed into the Earth from your feet.

Now breathe the roots up, and back into your body just like the branches that were above you. Give yourself over to the total relaxation you now feel.

In a moment or two—and when you are ready—open your eyes.

Use the above Tree of Life Meditation to introduce calm and balance into your life.

As we come to the conclusion of this chapter, here are a few more thoughts about chakras, which function as our energy centers. When properly maintained, they produce healthy energy. It is this healthy energy that produces the physical body's aura. An aura is the energy your body radiates.

Having a weak aura or having bad spots in your aura usually means that one or more of your chakras are out of whack. A sick or weak aura screams that the person's chakras are not working properly; it is an indication that his or her chakras need work.

Meditation is important for replacing the stagnant energy in your body's chakras with clean-flowing energy. It is good not only for our aura but also for maintaining a healthy state of mind. Meditation flushes out unwanted, excessive, or negative energy with healing positive energy.

Consider a daily practice of The Tree of Life Meditation. You will find peace within yourself, and the world will look a little less hectic. This meditation lowers blood pressure and reduces stress. You can practice technique as often as you need it.

In Conclusion

This chapter we learned The Tree of Life Meditation. We also briefly discussed the Chakras.

Chapter Questions

1. What is an aura?
2. What does meditation do in terms of stagnant energy?
3. Through meditation, Wiccans can communicate with which beings?

CHAPTER 10:
GROUNDING

Imagine you're feeling upset and you'd really like to let go of built-up negative energy. Your answer is to ground yourself. Grounding is the process of giving up or getting rid of your negative and unwanted extra energy. This process sends this energy back to Mother Earth so that she may cleanse it and recycle it back into the universe.

For example, one year I had a particularly unpleasant conversation with my sweetheart. He was all stressed out about working hard at his job and doing our taxes paperwork. He wanted acknowledgment for all he was doing. But I was taking it as if he was blaming me for not doing enough.

After a few cross words, we retreated to different rooms. I wanted to ground myself, so I did a Tree of Life Meditation (described in the previous chapter). It worked. I returned to my sweetheart and hugged him. And we both went on to enjoy the rest of the evening.

Knowing how to ground successfully enhances our well-being. Grounding keeps us happy and healthy both physically and mentally. It cleans out our negative and unwanted energy. When used in conjunction with meditation, it is known as "Grounding and Centering."

Grounding Exercise

The simplest form of grounding is to place your hands on the bare Earth. Breathe in deeply. As you exhale, push your extra energy out of your body and into the Earth. As you do this, envision all the negative or excess energy in your body being taken back safely into Mother Earth for her to recycle and use as she needs. You should feel balanced and refreshed after doing your grounding exercises.

If this grounding exercise doesn't work for you, try hugging a tree. Trees are great at taking your unneeded energy and shunting it down safely into the Earth.

Practice grounding every day. You can ground yourself before going to work or school. Many Wiccans find it helpful to ground themselves before stepping inside their home, particularly if they have had a stressful day.

Before you enter your house, place your hands on the Earth to rid yourself of the negative energy you acquired that day. As an alternative, you may also take off your shoes and stand on the soil.

Remember to check how you are feeling throughout the day. If you need to ground, then do so. You'll find that grounding keeps you feeling refreshed and calm all day!

As we come to the conclusion of this chapter, I want to provide you with two scenarios in which grounding is very useful:

a) Sometimes, we have too much energy, even if it is positive energy. I recall the time I forgot to ground after a particularly rigorous ritual that left me with way too much energy. I was bouncing off the walls for days. You may think this is funny, but you try going to work with zero sleep!

b) Some forms of negative energy tax you with "weight" like a sack of cement. When you ground yourself, you release such energy, and you suddenly feel lighter and free. You will live a happier life.

Finally, the true benefit of grounding is to, in essence, refresh your energy. It's like having a river clear out a stagnant pool of water. Grounding truly is a cornerstone of Wiccan practice.

Chapter Questions
1) When should you do grounding?
2) How does grounding help you?
3) How often can you do grounding?

CHAPTER 11:
RAISING POWER

We raise power or energy to create positive change in ourselves and the world around us. It's the fuel that runs spells; it's the spark that propels our desires into reality.

We can raise power using many different techniques often during a ritual. This chapter discusses several popular methods.

The best way to prepare is to get in shape. A well-tuned body is a great powerhouse. I recommend cardiovascular exercise, which will help keep your heart pumping through some of the more arduous physical techniques described in this chapter.

Also, a fit body requires sufficient rest and a healthy diet. Your body needs proper fuel to raise the energy you want. I'm not talking about eating like a rabbit. Heck no! I am talking about moderation. Fruits, veggies and protein. Don't forget chocolate, the fifth food group.

A healthy and fit body will help you achieve your goal of raising enough power or energy to do your magickal work.

For those with health conditions or certain physical disabilities: Walking is a great low-impact exercise that can make a significant difference to your health. However, if walking is not a possibility, this chapter also includes power-raising techniques that don't require a lot of movement.

Be aware that your body is a temple to the Gods. They gave it to you.

Chanting

Chanting is a great way to create power. It can be combined with dance and other techniques (discussed below).

To begin, find a positive phrase tailored toward what you are trying to achieve. The phrase can be anything that works for you. I find that rhyming phrases have the best effect. Lines from your favorite poem are an excellent way to get started.

Here's an example:
Grant me wealth, and grant my wishes,
Stir it with a thousand kisses.

Concentrating on your phrase or short poem is the key to success. Repeating the phrase for a set number of times—such as thirteen or another number that means something to you—adds power to your spell or working. Once your energy is focused, stop chanting and release the energy into the universe to do its tasks.

Dance

Using dance to create energy is why exercise is so

important. Moving your body creates massive amounts of energy—and joy for that matter. But dancing can be a challenge if you are out of shape. You don't need to learn secret dance steps from ages long gone. Just move! Dancing in a circle is my coven's favorite way to raise power. It's even better if you have musicians to provide accompaniment.

If you're not in a coven, dancing alone works just fine. Consider chanting to make the music you need to dance. But if that doesn't work for you, put on a great CD and get movin'! Remember this is why the Gods created CD's and MP3's!

Drumming

Drumming works very well for raising energy. This combined with dancing is a sure winner in raising power. Drumming can be especially fun for those who are musically inclined. You can make up your own rhythms, whatever works best for you. Usually, one picks a regular beat like *hit*, pause, *hit*, pause and so forth. One usually beats in a constant and rhythmic fashion. Beating the drum faster or slower creates a different effect for the listener.

Wiccans find that they can effectively raise energy starting with a slower rhythmic beat, then, gradually increasing the rhythm until you are beating quite vigorously. This does a great job and drumming also combines (if you're the drummer) movement which can also help.

If you do not own a drum they are easy to find, and if you can't afford that you can make a simple drum or shaker out of household items. This can be fun if you like crafts because not only do you make your own drum or shaker, you can decorate it however you like.

Singing

Singing is a fun way to raise power. If you like to make up rhymes and lyrics this can really be enjoyable. You don't need to be able to sing like the current pop stars. Just let out your joy. The Gods do not judge someone by superficial things like perfect pitch. They want your passion and joy; if they're in your heart, then that is what counts.

If you can't write songs or chants, you can find great ones online. Try Googling "pagan chants" and see what you can find. Always remember the chant or song should mean something to you. If it doesn't, it will be harder to raise power than through one you really like. So be creative and have fun.

Breath Control

To bring power to your rites, use your breathing to control and draw energy up from the Earth and into your body. As you inhale, draw down energy from the sky into your body. Breath control not only cleans out negative energy, but it also pulls up positive energy.

As you may recall, we discussed the clearing of negative energy as part of the Tree Meditation in Chapter 9.

Breath control can also be combined with chanting. In fact, chanting goes hand-in-hand with most power-raising techniques.

Sex

Although many view sex as a sacred act unto itself, it is also a very powerful tool to raise power. Using sex for this purpose is considered an advanced tool. This technique is only used by consenting adults. Usually, these couples are spouses or dedicated partners.

Warning: Please note that no one should ever force or manipulate you into having sex with them. That is *not* the way. It is *not* possible to create any truly productive magick or power through coercion.

Power can only be raised when both parties get pleasure out of the sex act. Each needs to keep his or her partner in mind. Both must work together. Having said that, it can be a very powerful and beautiful means to raise power for your magickal workings. Also, don't forget about having sex with yourself. That works, too!

In Conclusion

You have learned a few of the many ways to raise power. Once you become adept at the techniques described here, you will discover even more methods to explore. But realize that any method you undertake will take time to perfect. So don't stress yourself out—just enjoy. And remember to ground the extra energy once you are done with it.

Chapter Questions

1. Name three ways to raise energy.
2. Which method or methods can be used together? Explain.
3. How do you use breath control?

CHAPTER 12:
CASTING CIRCLE

To practice magick, Wiccans use tools, altars, grounding exercises, and the practice of raising power or energy. Rituals combine all of these pieces into one harmonious rite. The casting of a circle is where it all comes together.

When first casting circles, I felt nervous about making a mistake. I cast my first circles when I was a solitary witch. Soon I gained some confidence while becoming more and more familiar with the process.

The casting circle is valuable because it's where your ritual work is practiced. The casting circle functions as the doorway between the worlds, both the mundane world and the spirit world. When you cast a circle, you create a temple of energy. This temple or circle is where you worship the Gods and Goddesses and work magick. The circle contains the energy raised by the practitioner(s) and prevents the energy's dissipation until it has been used. It also keeps out unwanted entities and, due to its sacred nature, aids the ritual work.

Casting a circle involves several steps. The following lays this out for you in detail. Refer to Chapter 7 for information about the tools you need and Chapter 8 for the proper setup of your altar.

Setup
Before you begin, you will need:

1) A table for the altar.
2) Candles and candleholders for the four directions in the colors that represent each (red for south, blue for west, green for north, yellow for east.)
3) A red candle for the God and a green candle for the Goddess. These candle colors are preferable but not mandatory. You may also use white candles, which represent all colors.
4) A working candle to represent the element Fire.
5) A cup or chalice.
6) An athame.
7) A sword. If you don't have one, use the athame to cast the circle.
8) Incense and incense burner.
9) A dish of salt, preferably sea salt.
10) A bowl of water.
11) A bell or chime.
12) An altar cloth to keep wax and the other things off the table.
13) Wine or juice and some sort of cake.
14) A lighter.
15) A taper (to light the other candles from the working candle).

Next, locate the four directions (north, south, east and west); you can use a compass. Wiccans divide the area of the circle into four parts ("quarters"), corresponding with the four directions. Place the "quarter candles" in their respective corners: green in the northern-most corner, yellow in the east, red in the south, and blue in the west.

The Script

Before you begin, ground and center using the Tree of Life meditation exercise (see Chapter 9). This will help to clean out and balance your energy. This vital step helps you get into the right frame of mind before you start.

Next, you need a script to cast a circle or temple for conducting harmonious rites. Don't worry if the rites you perform don't flow easily at first. You just need practice. Consider writing your own script to follow. This may make it less confusing for you.

The following is an example of a script you can use. The parts you say out loud are in bold. This makes it easier to be seen by candlelight.

Note: This script is written for someone who is casting alone.

1) Knock *three* times on the altar. Ring the bell *three* times.

2) Light the working candle with the lighter and put it down on the altar. (The other candles will be lit later using the taper.)

3) Light the charcoal (if you are using it) from the working candle. (The incense will placed on the charcoal later.)

4) Take your athame and place its tip into the flame of the working candle. Say:

   a. **I exorcise* you o creature of fire. And I consecrate and bless you in the names of the Goddess and the God that you are pure and clean.**

(*Note: When we speak of *exorcise* here, we are purifying the item by driving out any negative energies.)

5) Trace a pentacle (a five-pointed star) over the flame. Pick up the candle and raise it up above you and imagine the Gods' energy filling the flame. Place the candle back on the altar.

6) Take your athame and place its tip into the bowl of water. Say:

   b. **I exorcise you, o creature of water. And I consecrate and bless you in the names of the Goddess and the God that you are pure and clean.**

7) Trace a pentacle in the water. Pick up the bowl of water and raise it up above you and imagine your energy and the Gods' energy filling the water. Place the bowl back on the altar.

8) Take your athame and place its tip into the salt. Say:

   c. **I exorcise you, o creature of salt. And I consecrate and bless you in the names of the Goddess and the God that you are pure and clean.**

9) Trace a pentacle in the salt. Pick up the bowl of salt and raise it up above you and imagine your energy and the Gods' energy filling the salt. Place the salt bowl back on the altar.

10) Take your athame and place its tip into the incense. Say:

d. I exorcise you, o creature of Air. And I consecrate and bless you in the names of the Goddess and the God that you are pure and clean.

11) Trace a pentacle over incense. Pick up the incense and raise it up above you and imagine your energy and the Gods' energy filling the incense. Place the incense on the lit charcoal.

12) Take your athame and scoop up three blades of the salt. You may also use your finger. Put the three pinches of salt into the water and mix it with the blade of your athame to make consecrated water. Pick up the bowl of consecrated water and raise it up above you and imagine your energy and the Gods' energy filling it.

13) Take the consecrated water (the salt and water mixture) and dip your fingers into it. Dab some of it on your inner wrists and forehead. Say:

e. I bless myself with Earth and Water.

14) Take the censer filled with the burning incense and wave the smoke over you. Say:

   f. I bless myself with Air and Fire.

15) Take the consecrated water and use your fingers to asperge (sprinkle with consecrated water) the circle. Starting with north and moving clockwise, walk a complete circle around the perimeter, aspersing each corner as you go. When finished, place the bowl back on the altar.

16) Pick up the censer filled with the burning incense. Use your hand to wave the incense smoke around the circle. Starting with north and moving clockwise, walk a complete circle around the perimeter, waving the smoke as you go. Be careful not to burn yourself or anything else. When finished, place the censer back on the altar.

You have just cleansed the space and yourself. Now let's continue by casting the circle.

17) Take the athame. Envision energy being channeled from you and coming out the tip of your athame [You point the athame outward, away from you as you create the circle.] Starting with north and moving clockwise, walk a complete circle around the perimeter. As you walk, say:

   g. I conjure you, o circle of power, that you be a boundary between the seen mundane world and the spirit world, that you protect me and contain the magick that I shall raise within you! I

consecrate and bless you in the names of the Goddess and the God. So mote it be!

18) Finish at the east quarter (direction).

Now it's time to "call the quarters." (This refers to the four directions.)

19) Pick up the athame and the taper from the altar. Light the taper from the working candle. Go and stand in the east corner of where your circle boundary is. Starting with the east candle, say:

h. I summon, stir, and call you up, o mighty ones of the East, element of Air. Come guard my circle and witness my rite.

20) Trace a pentacle in the air with your athame. Then light the quarter candle for east. Say:

i. Hail and welcome!

21) Move clockwise to the south candle. Say:

j. I summon, stir, and call you up, o mighty ones of the South, element of Fire. Come guard my circle and witness my rite.

22) Trace a pentacle in the air with your athame. Then light the quarter candle for south. Say:

k. Hail and welcome!

23) Move clockwise to the west candle. Say:

l. **I summon, stir, and call you up, o mighty ones of the West, element of Water. Come guard my circle and witness my rite.**

24) Trace a pentacle in the air with your athame. Then light the quarter candle for west. Say:

m. **Hail and welcome!**

25) Move clockwise to the north candle. Say:

n. **I summon, stir, and call you up, o mighty ones of the North, element of Earth. Come guard my circle and witness my rite.**

26) Trace a pentacle in the air with your athame. Then light the quarter candle for north. Say:

o. **Hail and welcome!**

27) Return to the altar. Using the taper, light the Goddess candle, saying:

p. **Welcome, my Lady!**

28) Using the taper, light the God candle, saying:

q. **Welcome, my Lord!**

You have now completed casting your circle!

At this time you can do any working or communicate with the Gods through meditation.

Cakes and Wine Ceremony

After any ritual, it is important to replenish and ground your energy. Food and drink help to replenish the energy spent doing the working or ritual. Food also helps you to ground.

But first you must bless the sustenance. Begin with the wine or juice.

1) Take the cup from your altar and pour the wine or juice into it. Then take the athame and dip its tip into the wine or juice. Say:

r. As the athame is to the male, so the cup is to the female, and so joined bring union and harmony.

2) Pour some of your blessed wine or juice into the offering bowl or plate on your altar. Say:

To the Gods!

You can now partake of the beverage.

3) Take your athame and point it over the cake. Say:

Blessed be these cakes that they bestow health, peace, joy, strength, and that fulfillment of love that is perpetual happiness.

4) Take one of the cakes (or just a piece) and place it in the offering bowl or plate. Say:

To the Gods!

You can now partake of the blessed cakes.

Note that this ritual was written for someone practicing alone. If it is conducted in a group, pass around the cup and the cakes, each person taking a sip and one of or part of the cake. As each person passes the wine and cake, this is the process:

As you hand the cup to another, say:
May you never thirst.

The other person replies:
Blessed Be.

As you offer a cake, say:
May you never hunger.

The other person replies:
Blessed Be.

After everyone has had some cake and wine (or juice) in this part of the ceremony, ask for feedback from the group about how the ritual went. You can now talk about experiences you had during the ritual or bring up feedback about the ritual. Relax and enjoy the rest of the food and drink, which will ground and replenish your spent energies.

So, what do you do with the blessed offerings in the offering dishes? You certainly don't just throw it into the garbage! They are gifts to the Gods. Take them outside to your garden where you can leave it on the ground to help nourish the Earth.

If you do not have a garden at your home, you can take the offerings out into the woods and leave them there. Some Wiccans who live in the city set the blessed offering out on their porch for local animals to partake. Be sure to only leave biodegradable food. Avoid wrappers or containers that will not decompose.

Closing Circle

It is very important to dismiss the energies you have called for your circle. Be sure to take down the magick temple (circle) you erected. And certainly dismiss the quarters!

If you forget to do these crucial steps, mishaps are sure to happen. It would be like telling the Elementals, "Make yourselves at home!" And they will. Elementals are not bad or evil; it's just that they can be mischievous. Fire Elementals will start fires! Water Elementals might mess with your plumbing. They don't act out of malice, but causing problems seems to be in their nature. They are great allies when practicing magick, but they need to go home when you are done. So please remember to dismiss them.

To close your circle:

1) Take your athame and hold it up and stand facing the east. Say:

s. **Hail mighty ones of the East, the element of Air. I thank you for guarding my circle and witnessing my rite. May you depart to your fair and lovely realms. I bid you hail and farewell!**

2) Trace a pentacle in the air with your athame.

3) Continuing, moving in a clockwise circle, stand facing the south. Say:

  t. **Hail mighty ones of the South, the element of Fire. I thank you for guarding my circle and witnessing my rite. May you depart to your fair and lovely realms. I bid you hail and farewell!**

4) Trace a pentacle in the air with your athame.

5) Moving clockwise around the circle, stand facing west. Say:

  u. **Hail mighty ones of the West, the element of Water. I thank you for guarding my circle and witnessing my rite. May you depart to your fair and lovely realms. I bid you hail and farewell!**

6) Trace a pentacle in the air with your athame.

7) Moving clockwise around the circle, stand facing north. Say:

  v. **Hail mighty ones of the North, the element of Earth. I thank you for guarding my circle and witnessing my rite. May you depart to your fair and lovely realms. I bid you hail and farewell!**

8) Trace a pentacle in the air with your athame.

9) Return again to face east. While walking the boundary of the circle, say:

w. Fire seal the circle round,
Let it fade beneath the ground,
Let all things be as they once were before.
The circle is now no more,
Merry meet, merry part,
And merry meet again!
So mote it be!

Generally, the above is how to close a circle. However, each coven or practitioner may have slightly different variations on wording. Yet the process remains the same.

Simple Cleansing and Dedication Ritual for Your Tools

In this section, we will explore a simple ritual to cleanse and dedicate your tools.

First, realize that cleansing and dedication steps are best done before you use your tools. The process only needs to be done once.

If you want to cast a circle and you have not consecrated your athame yet, you can cast a circle using your finger like an athame. Once you have cast the circle and have done a cleansing ritual on the athame, then you can cleanse the rest of your tools with the consecrated athame.

1) Cast your circle. (See instructions above.)

2) Pick up the tool (an athame, wand, chalice, or whatever you are cleansing) to be dedicated. Sprinkle the consecrated water you made on the tool. Say:

    a. **I exorcise thee, o (name of tool), that I cleanse and consecrate you with Earth and Water.**

3)   Place the consecrated water down.

4)   Take the tool and place it over the burning incense and let the smoke from the incense waft over the tool. Say:

    a. **I charge and bless you with Fire and Air, and I here do dedicate this (name of tool) in the names of the Goddess and the God.**

5)   Now you can do the cakes and wine ceremony.

6)   Lastly, close the circle.

7)   That's it. You're done!

In Conclusion

In this chapter you learned how to conduct rituals, which can be modified to fit Sabbats as well as when casting spells and other rituals during Esbats. I encourage you to customize the scripts provided above to make them your own. This is another thing that is great about Wicca: Wicca is a living religion (like a living document). You have the power to adapt rituals to your taste.

Chapter Questions
1. What is the first step in creating a circle?
2. What is the purpose of the cakes and wine ceremony?
3. What Elements are used in the casting the circle ritual?

CHAPTER 13:
MAGICK, A HOW-TO GUIDE

In this chapter we will explore what magick is and different ways to practice it. Let's start with a quote from Heinrich Cornelius Agrippa (1486-1535), who wrote books on occult philosophy:

"Unless a man be born a magician, and God have destined him even from his birth to the work, so that spirits do willingly come of their own accord - which doth happen to few - a man must use only of those things herein set down, or written in our other books of occult philosophy, as means to fix the mind upon the work to be done; for it is in the power of the mind itself that spirits do come and go, and magical works are done, and all things in nature are but as uses to induce the will to rest upon the point desired."

From the above quote, we realize that most of us need to study (including "books of occult philosophy") and practice. Only some are gifted "from his/her birth to the work." We must be diligent in our study and practice of magick. What exactly is magick? Magick (with a "k") is the practice of using the natural energies, the Earth, and heavenly bodies to create change in oneself and the environment.

As we do magick, we guide the natural energies around us. These natural energies are within us, around us, everywhere and at all times, from an old-growth forest to your office cubicle in the big city. What are these energies? They are the energies of the elements and the universe. As you learned in Chapter 6, the building blocks for all things are the Five Elements: Air, Fire, Water, Earth, and Spirit. Life can't survive without each of these. Because of this, everything exudes energy, including trees, the sun, rocks, and ourselves.

We use the Five Elements' energies and the other energies to help us create change in our lives. During rituals, we can also ask the Gods for help by lending us their energy. But for now let's talk about the energies around us.

Energy & Magick

Note of caution: When doing magick, always use the energies around you. Never use your personal energy. The idea is to pull in other energy instead of just relying on your own energy.

During rituals we raise energy, channel it through our bodies, and direct it through our will. Chapters 9 and 11 give instructions on how to achieve these goals. They explain how to raise and work with the energy around you, and how to channel the energy through your body. Chapter 9 provides meditation exercises in which you draw up energy from the earth, and Chapter 11 explains how to raise the energy needed to do magick. Raising energy is like charging a battery.

Your body is like a battery, like a conductor for power or energy. As I mentioned, you never want to use your own personal energy when practicing magick. Doing so will run down your body or your battery.

Instead, you raise energy and use this energy to power your spells and work. You direct the energy to do its purpose by focusing and willing it. (Soon, in the paragraphs below, I'll explain the process of concentration.)

How Magick works

Without the necessary knowledge, spells fail. I've seen friends disappointed as their spells went wrong. We notice that many people buy a book of spells and cast away, not knowing the how and why. Spells will do a giant belly flop on you if this is what you do without the knowledge of how magick works in the first place.

Intent

To do successful magick, you need to understand several things. First, you must have an intent. You need to know what you want to manifest. I know this sounds simple, but many people just don't think the intent through.

Let's say you want a car. Okay, why do you want a car? Is it to take you to your job? Or is it something you want to have people envy? Hey I don't judge. But if you just say "I want a car" to the universe, you are likely to get that Pinto down the block.

Let's say you just moved to a new area and you need a car to get you around. You want something nice but economical. You don't want a piece of junk that will break down on you every chance it gets. I suggest you go shopping, whether it be on the internet or at a car lot. Get to know what you want and like for your car.

When you pick out features, you're attaching specific desires to the car. This will help manifest the car you want versus the junk heap down the block. Refine your image of the perfect car in your mind. Include other requirements you have like good gas mileage and inexpensive repair costs. The more specific you are with your intent, the less there will be unexpected results like getting the lemon down the lane.

Having a solid intent is your first step before you do any magick. Once you have that cornerstone set you can continue with the second thing which is concentration. During your spell you will need lots of concentration and visualization.

Visualization

We'll continue with the process of manifesting a particular car. You can use a toy car as a visualization focus object. As you stare at the toy car, you also use your mind to imagine getting into a real car and driving it. You can even take a number of steps further. For instance, if you desire a convertible car, you imagine the wind blowing through your hair as you drive with the top down.

Concentration

This is the process of focusing and then refocusing your mind on your visualization task. In essence, you concentrate on the object and on the images in your mind that are specific for your desired manifestation. It is natural for the mind to wander at times. When it does, you just consciously redirect your mind to focus on the visualization object once again.

Meditation

Some Wiccans begin with meditation to clear the mind before using both concentration and visualization. Let's return to the Tree of Life Meditation we covered in Chapter 9. Remember that you combined a focus on your breath with envisioning energy blossoming from your head as branches and from your feet as roots. (For specifics, return to Chapter 9).

Once you have cleansed your energy via the Tree of Life Meditation, you will focus on a shape—that is, a mental image of a shape (perhaps, a triangle or sphere). Using your mind's eye, view the shape from every angle. Concentrate on this shape for an extended time.

Willpower

The Collins English Dictionary defines willpower as "the ability to control oneself and determine one's actions."

Kelly McGonigal, Ph.D., author of *The Willpower Instinct*, wrote: "Willpower is about harnessing the three powers of I will, I won't and I want to help you to achieve your goals (and stay out of trouble)."

When it comes to successfully performing magick, willpower, to me, means the driving force of desire for some form of change. So I focus on the power of "I will." This is an important distinction because many people think of willpower as only the ability to avoid temptation.

The compelling observation is that Wiccans, who become proficient at these three processes of visualization, concentration, and meditation, actually strengthen their will.

How? Once you do the three processes, you actually enhance your belief, and you push through your doubt.

Realize, you need to *will* something into being. This includes confidence that what you are doing will work. If you don't have that, your spell just won't become a reality.

You need your will for your intent to be as strong as possible. This is why when we are desperate for something, we can usually manifest it. Using your will is deeply rooted in your desire. Lack of will just creates another belly flop.

I've now shared with you the five *must-haves* (intent, visualization, concentration, meditation and willpower) for doing magick that works.

Now, let's talk about some of the other tools we use to manifest our desires.

When you start to create a spell, you begin with the intent. Once you have that strongly in place, you start crafting the wording of the spell. Be specific, and in this way you will avoid loopholes or misunderstandings in your magick. Vague wording leads to mistakes and disappointment. Remember, if you merely ask for a car, you might get one that is a piece of junk.

Another tool for working magick is using herbs that attract a particular thing or effect. For example, to attract money, Wiccans often use cinnamon. They also use sage for purifying spaces, people, and more.

I would suggest keeping things simple, at least to start with. Simple spells can be the most potent because they are easy to do.

An example of a simple technique is to appease the Younger Self, which can be considered one's inner child. The Feri (Fairy) tradition calls this part of ourselves "Sticky Self." The Younger Self (inner child) likes to play. Younger Self likes song, dance, rhyme, and all the sparkly shiny things in life. She/he likes rattles and other objects which we can use as tools to connect with Younger Self.

Why am I talking about Younger Self? Wiccans use Younger Self as a messenger to the Gods. You need to keep Younger Self's attention so that she/he gets the message right. This may sound silly, but doing things that would keep a five-year-old happy in your magick is a good start. This is one reason why we use feathers, incense, candles, and other tools in our magick. There are other reasons, too. Everything has its own energy and meaning. Such energy and meaning help you focus and add power to the work that you do. Don't forget this is work. It takes a lot of energy and concentration to do spell work and magick in general.

So you have your intent and your words in rhyme. You have added other elements to make Younger Self happy and to lend extra meaning/power to your magick. At this point, once you have gathered all that you need, you cast circle. Do the spell by using your items to focus on your intent. Chant your words and use a power-raising technique (all while keeping keen concentration on your intent).

The next step is important. Without this step, you might as well not have done all the previous efforts. What step am I talking about? You need to let all that energy you raised and all that focus go. That's right, you need to release it into the universe so that it can do the job you set it out to do. This lets Younger Self carry your message to the Gods and to create the change you desire.

We will continue to talk about spells and their wording below.

The Tools of Magick

We don't really need anything but our own bodies to do

magick, although most Wiccans use props/tools/elements such as candles and incense to help with the process. Many of us need these tools to help us channel (focus) our raised energy or power toward the task we need to accomplish.

Doing magick is not all about the physical tools of the trade. If you read the old grimoires (textbooks about magick), you know that they talk about consecrated swords and pentacles and using hard-to-get incense and herbs. But the old masters knew that the most potent tool in your toolbox is your mind. Still, Younger Self really likes the material objects!

How do we awaken and use our minds? It's all about motivation and determination! It's about how emotionally connected and invested you are. You will receive the best results if you feel strongly about what you are working toward.

How invested are you? Remember we talked about intent, concentration, and will. Do you meditate and study on your desire, or do you go shopping instead? Do you buy a book on the subject, or do you go to a bar with your friends?

Take some time to clear your mind before you begin doing magick. I know this from experience. One time I did a ritual to increase prosperity, but my mind was still full of fear. Not only did the prosperity ritual fail to work, things went the other way! I actually lost some money to a mix-up at the bank!

So make sure to clear your mind and put yourself into a calm state of being. After you have done this, think about what you want to accomplish. Then concentrate your mind on your desire. Write it down to help clarify and solidify it. Focus on the essence of your work and narrow it down to a simple chant or phrase that you can concentrate on during your magick work.

The Clause

I find it very important to include the clause "an it harm none" (from *The Wiccan Rede*) at the end of the spoken spell. I also include it at the end of spells that are only written down and never used. There is a good reason for this: Words matter. It keeps the spell from harming you or anyone else. Also, it's just not possible to see the many ripples a spell might produce. Even the most carefully worded spell could have unforeseen effects, and may include an undesired negative result. Wording and intention are the keys to doing magick successfully.

Clarity of purpose is paramount. A spell that says, "I want more money in my life" is an open-ended statement. Try asking in a more specific way, like, "Let money find me in any way legal, with ease, love, and luck for me and everyone involved around me." Close your request with a clause like "an it harm none" or "for the good of all involved." This will guide your magick toward a successful outcome that will benevolent toward everyone involved.

Ethics

Let's examine some ethics of magick. As first discussed in Chapter 1, "an it harm none" is the law of Wicca. It doesn't only apply to the physical mundane world; it also applies to the unseen and magickal work we do as well.

Remember that all actions, whether physical or astral, will come back to us: We do not steal, or we will have things stolen from us. We do not do baneful (harmful) magick for the same reason: Whatever we send out will come back to us.

Here's a test. See what your first response is. A discussion follows each question.

Question 1: Can you do a healing spell on a sick friend who doesn't know about it?

Discussion: The rule is this: If your friend doesn't know about your intention to do a spell, then he/she hasn't given you permission to do it. This is a big NO! You always need to ask permission before working any magick on someone. And be forewarned that it is harmful to do magick on someone who feels it goes against their beliefs.

Question 2: Can you do a spell to make your boss give you a promotion?

Discussion: The best way to explore this is to present a scenario about "Susan." Her boss plans to give a promotion to either her co-worker John or her co-worker Terry. Susan has heard that she is not in the running. But she really wants the extra money that comes with the promotion. Susan does a spell and gets the promotion. But then both John and Terry are in terrible accidents.

Or, let's say nothing like that happens to John and Terry. Susan's boss merely changes her mind and suddenly decides to give the promotion to Susan. The problem is that Susan's responsibilities increase ten-fold. She no longer has time for friends or to take a weekend off. Then she finds out that Terry really needed the promotion to pay hospital bills and John ended up losing his house because he couldn't make the payments.

The answer here is: It is unethical to force someone to do something against his or her will, and this often create extreme, negative consequences.

Question 3: Can you do a love spell on your sexy neighbor to make him or her fall in love with you?

Discussion: Remember: Wiccans never work magick on someone against his or her will. Doing so is harmful. Do not forget the Law of Three. The violation of the Law will turn around and bite you on your ass!

The answer here is: Some misguided people do inappropriate love spells, anyway. They get overwhelmed when the target person falls desperately in love so much so that he or she starts following them everywhere. Soon spell-caster is stalked at work, at school, and at home. This scenario can become dangerous.

Never, ever do a love spell on a particular person! If you want to do a spell to draw love to you, that's fine. Make it general and do not target a specific person. This leaves space for the person to make choices by his or her own free will. Free will is crucial. Don't perform magick that interferes with a person's free will. Taking control of someone's decision making is baneful magick. Do NOT do it!

A Word on Offerings

Why do we give offerings and what are they?

Offerings are small gifts we present to the Gods. They can be many things from candles to wine. You can even offer up your time to a good cause for a deity. I used to volunteer at an animal shelter, for example. More often I offer candles and incense up as offerings. I take a candle and hold it up and say something like: "Here is a candle, please take this offering as thanks for _____."

Then I light the candle and place it on my alter to burn down completely. Never extinguish a candle once you have lit it for an offering to the Gods. This is considered taking back the gift and is insulting to the deity. Always let it burn down completely down and out on a safe heat proof surface.

You can also do this process with incense and other herbs. Burn incense and or herbs to the Deity you want to honor. Besides burning candles, incense and herbs you can pour a libation (a liquid offering) out onto the earth. You can use anything: wine, juice and blessed water.

Why do we present offerings to the Gods? We say thank you for the Gods help on things we have asked for. After a spell is successful, we will make an offering to say thank you for their help.

Some Popular Offerings:

- candles
- incense
- wine
- herbs
- seeds
- ground corn
- hand made objects
- fruit
- milk
- bread (cakes)
- time (volunteering at an organization)
- crystals
- coins
- donations of clothes or other things to a shelter (animal or human)

So say thank you to the Gods.
They help us every day.

The Moon and Magick

The moon greatly influences magick. The moon also influences our daily lives as well as the world around us. Consider how the tides ebb and flow with the moon's dance across the sky.

The moon's impact on water is well known. Yet many aren't aware of the extent that humans—who are about 60% water—are influenced by the moon. It's interesting to note that a woman's menstrual cycle is usually 28 days, about the same amount of time it takes the moon to circle the Earth (27.3 days, to be exact).

Next we will discuss the two cycles of the moon: the waxing (full) moon and the waning (dark) moon. Wiccans incorporate these two cycles in how they practice magick. Each cycle has its own energies that are used in different ways.

Waxing / Full Moon (Bright Moon)

Waxing is when the dark moon begins to reveal the light of her face. This cycle continues and increases until the moon's face is totally illuminated by the sun, when the moon is completely full or bright. Remember it this way: waxing is dark to light.

Wiccans practice most of their magick during the waxing. The brighter or fuller the moon, the more powerful her energies. It's during this "growing" of the light (waxing) that witches do magick for increase. For example, to increase one's wealth or to improve one's health. Doing a prosperity spell during the waxing moon says you want your prosperity to grow like the moon's brightness. The fuller the moon, the more potent its energy. A moon at its fullest increases a spell's power and its likelihood to succeed.

One April day during the waxing cycle, I did candle magic to draw money to me. Soon I received money from three unexpected sources. One was so surprising that I asked the person, "Did you give me the wrong envelope?" She replied, "No, we just wanted to show how we appreciate what you do."

Waning / New Moon (Dark Moon)

Waning is when the face of the bright moon begins to dim. The moon wanes or decreases from a full moon to completely dark. Such a dark moon is known as the new moon. Remember it this way: Waning is light to dark.

Wiccans use the waning cycle as the best time for magick work for decrease; for example, to lose weight or to get rid of a cold. Note that you can heal during both the waxing and waning cycles. The waxing moon helps draw back your health. The waning moon helps rid you of something unwanted, such as a cold or flu.

Warning: No magick is done on during the new moon phase, when the moon is completely dark in the sky. Witches should never touch the dark moon's energies. The energy of the dark moon is baneful. Never do any magick at this time; nothing good can be made from it. Avoid this phase of the cycle.

Magick and Prosperity-Money Magick

"If you're a witch and magick is real, why aren't you rich?" A simple, but valid question. So why are many Wiccans and magickal people in general struggling so much with money? One answer is: Many of us see a focus on money as un-spiritual. We do not see it as part of a spiritual path.

Have you noticed that many of us struggle for our daily needs of food on the table and a roof over our heads? Priests and priestesses focus on helping others. But many ignore money until they're struggling. Then money, or really the lack of money, monopolizes their attention. When that happens, they cannot help others. Having money, while not the most important thing in life, is valuable—like oxygen.

Being wealthy not only serves us in the materialistic world, but creates spiritual well being. How? Wealth, or abundance, creates a peaceful space in which you can breathe easy and even help others. With this understanding, it's truly helpful to incorporate money into our spiritual practice.

Here is a powerful idea: *using magick to help us gain wealth assists us to fulfill our spiritual needs.* Again, I am talking about abundance. When you experience abundance and take care of your financial needs, you do something truly valuable: you remove the distress that many people feel about money. Such distress is so distracting that it takes up too much energy and can make people feel miserable. Wouldn't it be better to have your financial needs fulfilled and to even have an abundance of financial and other blessings? Why? Because you can *share with others* from a place of personal strength and wholeness.

An important note: let's focus on the idea that we're encouraged to do what is necessary to create financial abundance *on the physical plane.* Many Wiccans have regular jobs or serve others through their efforts as business owners. You do *not* have to use magick to gain money and financial abundance.

Here's another way to look at it. You can eat a healthy diet for your physical health. You may not absolutely need vitamin supplements. But why take a chance? Personally, I eat well *and* take vitamins. Don't you?

Similarly, you could *try* to keep your job and other money-generating activities separate from your spiritual life. But why not incorporate how you serve others (that's what you're doing when you work in your own business or for an employer) *into* your spiritual life?

Doesn't it make sense to develop a spiritual life that includes abundance and wealth? By the way, I notice that some Wiccans feel *more comfortable* about doing a spell for "transportation" which provides for the possibility that one gets a pass for using public transportation or that a relative gives a castoff old car. *That is fine.* We can ask whether it's okay to *also have more options* that money can provide.

You notice I used the word wealthy earlier and not "rich." I purposely use the word "wealthy." So what's the difference? Rich is the flow of money coming in; wealth is a state of having money. I think author Jason Miller says it well:

> A rich person has a high income, which is a stream that can feed being wealthy or being in debt, depending on how that money is used. There is no shortage of people with high incomes but no real wealth. . . . Wealth is not a flow of income; it is a state of positive finances.

I've talked with some Wiccans who say that when money is tight, they use magick to pay the rent or a credit card bill. And this works. However, too often we ask magick to fix our problems when these difficulties have grown too large. We wait until we have no other option than to use our magick. We come from a place of desperation instead of a place of balance.

Again, I want to share that it's healthier to take care of money-related concerns so that you do not "just get by." Instead, you do what is necessary to *enjoy abundance* and balance. Ideally, Wiccans use magick to get to an inner state where they work out problems that prevent them from enjoying such abundance. For example, some Wiccans may do many prosperity spells but perhaps, would benefit more for a *healing spell* so that they learn to *save money and improve their spending habits.*

The first step for using magick effectively for financial well-being is to work our magick in a consistent manner not only to sustain us but also to build something more out of our money.

Too often we use magick to maintain where we are at, and we don't use magick to build us up to where we want to go.

So it seems practical to use magick to create sustained wealth. The question is: What can magick do, and what can't it do? Jason Miller suggests, "Practical magic can do two things: it can affect the minds of other people; and it can shift probability in your favor, making improbable things more probable."

This sounds good. However, we must take care and remember The Law of Three—what you send out returns to you with three times the force. Remember, messing with someone's free will is *simply wrong,* and it will likely cause havoc in your life.

So what is the proper use of magick? It is a measured use. For example, for a job interview, you can devise a spell that includes the words: "May I be at my best during my interview. May the interviewer be feeling well during our time together. May the interview turn out for the good of all involved."

Do you notice how you are not trying to force the situation and push the interviewer to hire you, even if you are not the ideal candidate in their mind? The Gods may see that this job is not ideal for you, and you may not be seeing it.

Your spell does not conflict with the Gods protecting you from an inappropriate employment situation.

Get Clear About Wealth

It's reported that Buckminster Fuller said the wealth can be measured in the number of days that one can live one's normal lifestyle without a paycheck.

So it's not the amount that comes in that is the key; it's how much you keep and use to build your abundant finances. We're not talking about becoming misers. Money needs to flow in order to work. Think of it like water: it needs to flow and move, or it gets stagnant and bad. Money needs to flow in cycles. Author Larry Winget said, "When you share what you have earned with others, then it magically comes back to you. I don't know why it works, but it works."

So having wealth is what we need, not just being rich. And to experience true wealth, we have money flow in our lives like water. This is where magick comes in.

Let's focus on avoiding the big mistake—using spells the wrong way, that is, doing spells and magick only when we are desperate for money.

Instead, create a healthy relationship with money. A healthy relationship is not one in which a partner only comes to the other person during times of desperation. You build the relationship day by day and year by year.

On the other hand, here is an example of taking a desperate approach toward increasing one's income. One year, I sought to increase my abundance. I, like many others, only asked for financial help when I was in trouble. I would do a spell here and there, seeking a windfall or at least something to get me by.

With this mentality, most of my money spells at that time would fail. Once it even backfired on me. I had done an elaborate spell to seek help for improving my finances. It was the same month that a large portion of my income suddenly dried up. It felt like my magick had turned against me.

I thought long and hard about it. Slowly I began to realize my mistake. I needed wealth not "quick money." So I did a different spell. Instead of asking for prosperity to simply drop into my lap, I asked that it be returned to me in whatever legal means possible and that I have the energy to accomplish the necessary actions to bring in income.

So I did a spell to ask for the strength and energy that I needed to create my own financial wealth. I realized that I was my own source of energy and that I was the one to create the money I desired. As I continued doing spells toward my goal, I didn't concentrate on the money aspect of it. I concentrated on the end result. I concentrated on how I could build on what I did have to create wealth in my life.

This is what happened. Every week I would honor the Gods with an offering of incense or by burning a candle to them. I thanked them for their guidance in this new endeavor and for helping to build my capabilities to accomplish my goal of wealth. I did another spell, keeping in mind my goal, and I continued to burn offerings to the Gods.

Several weeks went by. Then one night I awoke with a wild idea: I needed to write a book. So the next day when I got up, I could hardly contain all the excitement and energy I had for the plan. I had even dreamt up a title in my sleep. I checked online to see if it was available, and it was. I knew then that the Gods were guiding me, and this was what they wanted for me. My first step was to begin a blog. My initial concern was that my dyslexia would hinder my attempt to write. I figured that writing a blog would help get my feet wet.

So I started www.TheHiddenChildrenoftheGoddess.com. I now know that I will be just fine. I know that my writing will help others as well as myself. When you write a book, you naturally dig deeper and learn during your journey of writing. And the book I was guided to write is this book in your hands now.

I continue to give the Gods offerings of thanks, and I ask for their continued guidance.

Colors and Candle Magick

Let's begin with the meanings of the different candle colors.

Note that the following list is not the final word on color. For instance, the color blue may have another meaning to you than the one listed here. Remember that your mind is your greatest tool. Trust your instincts when your feelings about a specific color differ from what others may advise you.

Here is a list of colors and a brief summary of their general attributes.

- Red: sex, desire, vitality, strength
- Orange: charm, confidence, joy, jealousy, persuasion
- Yellow: intellectual development, joy, intellectual strength
- Green: prosperity, abundance, fertility, money matters
- Blue: healing, protection, spiritual development
- Purple: the occult, power, magick
- Pink: love, friendship, compassion
- White: purity, innocence, peace, tranquility, and
- Black: decrease, death, revenge, retribution, contacting the dead

Note: I *strongly* recommend that you *never* use a black candle. The exceptions are at Samhain or when talking to the dead. Remember the Law of Three!

A candle that has been used for a specific purpose should never be used for a different purpose. Also, it is preferable to burn down the candle all the way. Try to do this in one session. Otherwise, it is acceptable to use the same candle again—but only for the same spell.

Candle Spell

Candles are a great way to do magick. It's fun and relatively simple to do, and chances are good that you'll get positive results. The following spell can be modified for different purposes.

To get started, get a new slip of plain paper with no lines. Concentrate on your desire until it is clear in your mind. Write it down. Rework it as much as needed. The process of writing your desire on paper will help manifest what you want to happen. Also, writing it down helps clarify and focus your will. This paper will be used in the spell.

What you will need to conduct a candle spell:

- Your altar
- A fireproof surface (perhaps, a plate) added on top of your altar
- Your magick tools (including your athame, candle holders, etc.)
- A script to use as you cast your circle
- The piece of paper upon which you wrote your desire
- A pen or pencil
- A candle of appropriate color for the spell (use a small taper candle or tealight because this candle will need to be burned completely)
- Cakes and wine or juice for the ritual
- A fireproof container

To cast a candle spell:
1) Cast your circle.

2) Take the paper with your desire inscribed. Asperge and cense (waft incense smoke around) it.

3) Select the candle color that's appropriate for what you need. Asperge and cense the candle (which we now the "spell candle").

4) Dress your spell candle.

To dress the spell candle means: The process of putting your desire into the candle. As you clearly envision your wish, rub anointing oil (olive oil will suffice) on the candle. Spread the oil from the top of the candle to the center, and then from the bottom back to the center. Rubbing from each end of the candle to the center draws or attracts a desire to you. If you wish to repel something, for example an illness or bad luck, you would rub from the center out to each end of the candle. This pushes away what you wish to repel.

5) Charge the paper with its task by reading it over and over. Read out loud or silently to yourself. It is important to concentrate on the desire. Take your time with this step.

6) Place the paper on your altar.

7) Light the spell candle with the working candle. Place the paper under the spell candle.

8) Look at the flame of the spell candle while concentrating on your desire. Take your time with this step.

9) Raise energy. Chant, do breath control, or dance around the spell candle. Whichever method you choose is fine, or use a mixture of methods. Just be sure to keep your desire firmly in your mind while you do it. You should start to feel the energy flow as you continue to raise power. (This is where a coven comes in handy.)

10) When you feel you have raised enough energy, focus the energy into the flame and down the spell candle

into the piece of paper under it. This step calls for you to envision the energy you raised to flow down the spell candle.

11) Take the paper from under the lit spell candle and then carefully ignite the paper using the spell candle's flame.

12) Place the burning paper into a flameproof container to allow it to burn completely, letting the smoke go up to the Gods. Many witches use a cauldron for this purpose.

13) Let the spell candle burn down completely—in a safe place. Do not leave the room.

14) After the spell is finished, do the cake and wine/juice ritual. And don't forget to ground yourself when you are finished. You must send the extra energy down into the Earth.

15) Close your circle.

How to Do a Prosperity Spell

You can use this prosperity spell if you need money in a flash. Prosperity spells can be tricky, though. You need to be specific so that you do not have undesired effects. Be open enough in your wording to let money come to you from places and opportunities you may not have thought of yet. Here is a simple spell that fits these requirements.

Let's talk about the wording of this spell so you can see how it works.

The first line is:

Grant me wealth, and grant my wishes,
stir it with a thousand kisses.

This line states the purpose and the way you want your desire to come to you. "With a thousand kisses" means with only love. You make sure that wealth does not come with pain or trouble for anyone.

The second line states:

By the moon, and by the sun,
watch for it, 'cause here it comes

This line uses the powers of the moon and the sun to help accomplish your desire.

The third line says:

It comes by night, it comes by day,
it comes to me with no shades of gray

By mentioning both night and day, the line communicates the intention is that wealth arrives continually.

The phrase "it comes to me with no shades of gray" is very important. The idea of "no shades of gray" means you want wealth to come to you without any negativity associated with it. For example, you want that no one will get into an accident and leave you money.

The fourth line finishes with:

The sea goes in, the sea goes out,
now look at me, my wealth about!

This last line talks about the outcome of the spell. You affirm that you do receive wealth.

The fifth line is simple:

So mote it be!

This line activates the spell.

You can notice that this spell has the power of the five elements in it. I know it isn't obvious. I'll explain. The grant part in the first line comes from Spirit. This refers to your need. This desire arises from your heart. Here is where the process begins.

The second line talks about the heavenly bodies in the sky which is Air. You're placing your thought into the world.

The third line emphasizes no shades of gray or no shadows. Fire is light, and it chases darkness away, banishing the shadows from your wish.

The fourth line is a declaration of manifesting wealth. We can notice that *wealth*, in the Tarot, is symbolized as Earth. Further, "the sea goes in, the sea goes out" refers to Water and birthing wealth.

The last line "so mote it be" echoes the second line and plants the entire spell into reality. In effect, it fulfills the desire.

Now that we have discussed the spell and how it works, let's begin. Remember to cast your circle first. If you don't know how to do that read my how to cast circle chapter.

Elemental Money Candle Spell

What you will need:
- Candles in colors: white, yellow, red, blue, and green (representing the elements).
- Pentacle
- Matches or lighter
- Ritual tools

Place candles at appropriate elements on the pentacle (see special diagram below).

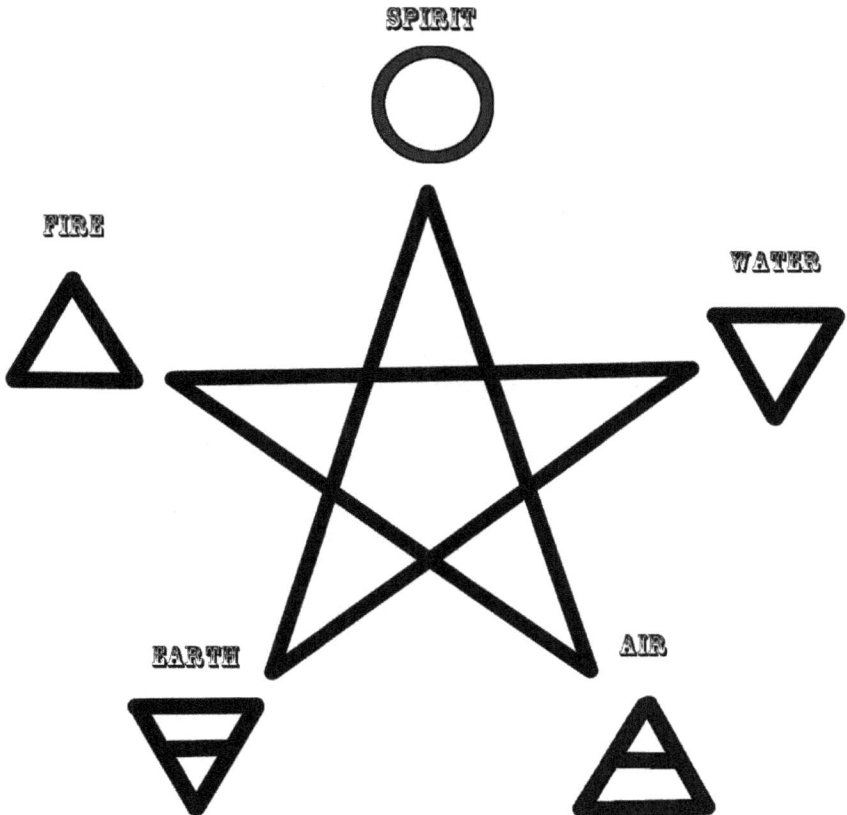

SPIRIT

FIRE

WATER

EARTH

AIR

1. Set up your altar and space. Then cast your circle
2. Do the spell

Say while lighting the white candle:

> **Grant me wealth, and grant my wishes,**
> **stir it with a thousand kisses.**

Light the yellow candle and say:

> **By the moon, and by the sun,**
> **watch for it, 'cause here it comes.**

Light the red candle and say:

> **It comes by night, it comes by day,**
> **it comes to me with no shades of gray.**

Light the blue candle and say:

> **The sea goes in, the sea goes out,**
> **now look at me, my wealth about!**

Light the green candle and say:

> **So mote it be!**

4. Do the Cakes and Wine Ceremony
5. Close the circle

Second Money Candle Spell

Here is another example of a simple candle spell you can use for prosperity.

What you will need:
- Your altar
- Your tools
- A script to cast your circle
- Cakes and wine or juice
- A green candle (green is for prosperity, although you may also use gold)
- Matches or a lighter
- Money Oil (oil designed to draw money to you—see below)

To make Money Oil, mix together the following essential oils:
- 1 part ginger
- 2 parts orange
- 1 part pine
- 2 parts cinnamon
- 1/2 part chamomile
- 1 part cedar wood
- 1 part jasmine (optional)

This spell should be done only on the waxing moon. The best time is when the moon is closest to being full.

To do this Money Spell:

1) Cast your circle.

2) Take one green or gold candle.

3) Dress your candle.
"Dress" the candle with the Money Oil. While envisioning money flowing into your life, rub the oil on the candle.

Spread the oil from the top of the candle to the center, and then from the bottom back to the center. This technique charges the candle with your will. So be sure to concentrate and take your time with this step.

4) Use the taper to light the green or gold candle from the working candle.

5) Concentrate on the flame. Put your will into it. Take your time.

6) Speak or chant the following:

As I light this candle so,
Make my money grow and grow.
Let it flow without rhyme or reason,
Each and every turn of season.
Filling up my pockets wide,
Let me enjoy this happy ride.
With no malice, woe, or hitches,
May there be no mess with glitches.
Let me have no need for fear of ruin,
Whilst letting go of poverty for fortune,
So mote it be!

Note: The following lines fulfill the "an it harm none" clause requirement mentioned earlier in this chapter: "No malice, woe, or hitches, May there be no mess or glitches" and "Let me have no need for fear of ruin."

Healing Candle Spell

Healing can be done in many ways. You can use herbs, colors, candles, and more.

The simplest way to do healing is to light a candle for a sick person. Wiccans use two parts to the process: Dressing the candle and stating the purpose for the use of the candle.

For the second part, you state the purpose of using the candle. Here is an example:

"I send healing energy to (name of person)."

Reminder about ethics and magick: When doing any spell work for another person, you must ask for their consent first. If you do not ask, you may be working against their will. So always ask first. One possible exception may be in the cases of coma, dementia or unconsciousness. In such a situation, you ask the universe for the best outcome for the person.

What you will need:

- Your altar
- A fireproof surface (perhaps, a plate) added on top of your altar
- Your tools
- Your written script of "words of power" (perhaps, a small prayer or rhyme talking about how the person is now healed)
- A script to cast your circle
- One blue candle (a small one because it will be burned down in one sitting)
- Dressing oil (you can use plain olive oil if you do not have any)
- Cakes and wine or juice for the ritual
- A fireproof container

- A photo of the sick person

To cast a candle spell:

1) Cast your circle.

2) Take the photo of the sick person. Turn the photo over and sprinkle just a little consecrated water on the edges of the photo. Then cense (waft incense smoke around) the photo.

3) Take the blue candle and asperge and cense it.

4) Dress your candle (see the discussion above).

5) Charge the candle with its task. (Send healing energy into the candle by holding it in your hands and drawing energy up through the earth, through you, and into the candle. The process of drawing energy up consists of visualizing energy (you might imagine energy strands) rising from the earth into your feet and so on.

6) Take the photo and place it on the pentacle on your altar.

7) Place the blue candle next to the photo. Use the taper to light the blue candle from the working candle.

8) Look at the flame of the blue candle while concentrating on your desire to heal the person. Take your time with this step. This is a great time to chant any words of power (if you have written some). Remember, these words of power could be a small prayer or rhyme talking about

how the person is now healed. During this time, you might ask the universe to bring healing to the person or you might ask for an insight about how to heal the person.

9) Keep focusing that energy into the flame of the blue candle and into the photo under it. (Focusing energy means keep concentrating on the flame and focus your thoughts on the intention that the person be healed.)

10) You will be letting the candle burn down completely. Warning: Use a fire safe container for the candle to be in, such as a bathtub or sink. Be sure to avoid leaving a candle unattended. That is, do NOT leave the room while your candle is burning down. And make sure that you do not burn the photo!

11) After the spell is finished, do the cakes and wine/juice ritual.

12) Close your circle.

Doing a healing ritual is empowering for the sick person, and it is also an uplifting experience for the practitioner. It feels good to be able to marshal the healing energies of the universe to bless the life of person who needs healing.

The Astral Body and the Astral Plane

So far we haven't talked about the astral body or plane. Wiccans believe in the astral plane. There your astral body lives. Many people understand the astral body can be seen as the aura of a person. The astral plane has many inhabitants besides your astral body. But that's for another book. Sometimes "things" can attach themselves to your aura in the astral plane. They tend to be vampiric and can feed on your astral body draining your body of its energy, even to the point of causing physical illness.

So the astral body is the subtle energy body of your physical body. Different traditions have different viewpoints on how many "layers" the astral body has. However, most practitioners agree we all have one. As Wiccans, we can modify the aura or astral body with the different healing techniques we use. Some of these include, but are not limited to, color magick, the chakras, spells and meditation. We will see an example of healing below with the spell/ritual called the *Separation Ritual*.

Many people have heard of astral projection. This is the practice of leaving your physical body (by way of your astral body) to go to another location on the astral plane. The astral plane is much like the world around us. There are astral representations of everything we see around us: trees, rivers, and animals. For the adept practitioner, when in the astral plane, she can change her surroundings at will, which can influence the physical world she lives in.

Is the astral plane good or bad? My answer is: it's neither. The astral plane has all sorts of entities that live there, just like the physical world around us. Some are very friendly and others, not so much. One thing I have noticed is that you attract the same energy that you put out into it. What does that mean? If you see disaster around every corner in the physical world, you will probably run into things that are attracted by that energy of "expecting something bad to happen." On the other hand if you are an optimist you will attract those kind of beings that like and give off that positive energy. Much of it depends on the mood of the person traveling on the astral plane.

Another thing: I carry my astral sword with me when I travel on the astral plane. My swords helps me protect myself if I ever run into something not so nice. I have the good fortune to tell you I have not needed to use it. However, a good friend of mine had to use her sword one time. She was attacked by a vampire on the astral plane and used her sword to vanquish the assailant.

So how do I get an astral sword? Building one in the astral plane is best. I made mine in a meditation.

You could begin with the image of an actual athame that you own. Realize that as soon as your athame had been blessed and consecrated it already had an astral form that can be used in the astral plane. Later, during a meditation (and on the astral plane), you could transform your athame into a sword (through your own thought). Remember that athames are never used to cut physical things. However, the astral plane is made up of *all energy*, so you can use an athame (in astral form) to cut the energy around you there.

In the astral plane we are all connected, like a spider web. Everything is connected in some way to everything else. However when we make friends and other bonds with people or animals we create an astral connection to them. These bonds can last a life time. Sometimes we prefer to sever such a bond because many of us have people who are toxic in our lives. In the below *Separation Ritual* I will show you how to release those unwanted ties by cutting them at the points where they attached to your astral body.

How to Heal by Separating Yourself Spiritually from a Bad Relationship

We've all been in a bad relationship at some time in our lives. Whether it is a family problem or ex-lovers or a friendship that just plain went sour. So how do we spiritually separate ourselves from these poisonous people?

You can use many different ways to accomplish this. However, the first and foremost thing to do is to verbally end the relationship. You might say something like: "I don't think this is healthy for us. So let's just stop seeing each other."

Second, physically stay away from the person. The idea is to stop spiritually ingesting the poison of interacting with them.

Many people hesitate to do the first two steps. For many, true change is quite difficult. I can relate to this. And, I'm providing the below ritual for when you're truly ready to move on with your life.

Now, it's time to use what I call the Separation Ritual. This ritual involves disconnecting the astral connections that you and the person made during the relationship.

Unless you take action, you stay connected to the person. How? Your astral bodies remain connected. Negative energy can still be transferred both ways. To protect yourself from these bad energies you must cut all ties from that person. This is where the Separation Ritual comes in.

Ideally, the person would participate in a Separation Ritual with you. That often does *not* happen. So you take an object that will *stand in* for the person. This object could be a picture or even a teddy bear, if the person likes teddy bears.

Use a length of yarn or piece of red string, which represents the connections you have between you and the toxic person. Red is for the life force but you can uses another color if you think that would be a better representation.

For this ritual you'll need both your athame (to cast your circle) and a boline, which is a white handle knife used specifically for cutting physical objects during ritual.

Important: Athames are used to cut energy. Bolines are used to cut physical objects.

Here are the steps of True Separation:
1. Verbally end the relationship
2. Stay away from the person.
3. Ground yourself.
4. Cast circle.
5. Do the Separation Ritual (see below).
6. Do the Cakes and Wine ritual.
7. Close the circle.
8. Finally continue to have no contact with the toxic person.

You will need your usual ritual items to cast circle and your altar. As I mentioned you will also have a length of yarn or piece of red string. The yarn/string must be long enough to encircle your own waist and to encircle the object (that represents the toxic person).

The Separation Ritual
Take the object. First, your will asperge it.

With the consecrated water, asperge and say:
I cleanse and consecrate you by water and earth.

Next you will cense the object. Cense means to waft incense smoke over the object.

With the incense smoke, cense and say:

I bless and charge you with air and fire.

Then take the string/yarn and cense and asperge it as well and say:

I cleanse and consecrate you by water and earth.
I bless and charge you with air and fire.

Take the red string/yarn in your hands saying:
Tiny bundle of String/yarn, You are now the same as the bonds between me and Name of person.

Tie one end of the string/yarn to the object and then encircle your waist with the other end of the string/yarn, while you say:
You _are_ the bonds that connect us now.
From me to <u>Name of person</u> and from <u>Name of person</u> to me. Our connection is by thee.

Sit and concentrate on the bond between you both and see it as the string/yarn that now connects you and the object. Once you have a firm connection with that thought, take the boline and cut the string/yarn, seeing in your mind's eye the astral bonds being cut along with the string/yarn.

Once you complete the cut, say:
I am now free of the ties of <u>Name of person</u> as he/she is of me. May my happiness expand, and may <u>Name of person's</u> happiness expand.
Blessed be.

Finish up with the cakes and wine part of the ritual and then close the circle.
And you're done.

Separating ourselves from toxic people is important for our happiness and well being. It even blesses the life of the other person. You are doing yourself and the other person a favor.

I trust that this ritual will help you be happier and healthier.

Color Magick for Healing

Which color do you prefer? Do you like the warmth of red? Maybe the coolness of blue? Or the royal luxury of purple?

I admit it: I like bright colors in the form of tie-dyed fabric. It's like the rainbow, but better because the colors mix in surprising patterns. I have tie-dyed shirts and skirts. And I'm considering tie-dyed drapes. This reminds me of the old Bill Cosby comment: "Any man who thinks he's the king of the castle, let him pick drapes by himself!"

Let's talk about how colors are made. There are two different color systems to look at. The first is the subtractive color system. Wiccans use the subtractive color system when they dye clothing, including robes. Sometimes they craft custom items for their altar.

Artists, such as painters, are most familiar with this type of system. So what is the subtractive system? When you add a pigment RYB (Red, Yellow, Blue) to a white piece of paper or canvas, you are blocking out the white, in effect subtracting it from what you see. This is the same process that color ink jet printers use with their color cartridges of CMYK (Cyan, Magenta, Yellow, Black.) They add ink to the page, tinting it to the appropriate hue. Each color can be added to the other to get a different color using the combination of the two.

Now we'll discuss the second system, known as the additive system. Light acts differently than pigments, so instead of the primary colors of CMYK for the subtractive system, you have RGB (Red, Green, and Blue) for mixing light. You'll notice there is no yellow. This is because yellow comes from a mixture of red and green. Try it. With the additive system, mixing all the colors together results in white light. On the other hand, adding all the colors in the subtractive system yields black. We will be working mostly with light, so we'll concentrate on the additive system.

Color comes from sunlight. You can use a prism to separate all the colors into a rainbow array of hues: red, orange, yellow, green, blue, indigo, and violet. Each color has its own wavelength or vibration/frequency. Red has a long or low frequency as opposed to violet's short wavelength or high frequency.

Having its own wavelength, each color has its own vibration, characteristics, and properties. This is the key. These vibrations, characteristics, and properties are what we use within magick.

How does this work? Everything from a rock, to a tree, to even you is made up of vibrating matter. Everything is made up of molecules. All molecules vibrate, and when we use the vibrations of different colors, we change the frequency of whatever we are working with. It's that simple. Author Charles Klotsche confirms: "Each color relates to a particular wavelength, or vibration, on the visible spectrum. ... These color vibrations, which can also be regarded as energies, can produce healing effects when the appropriate wavelengths (colors) are used."

So what about black and white? Black absorbs all the colors, and white reflects all the colors. So in the additive color system (remember we are talking about light), your aura would be all white. However this almost never happens. If a person's aura is black, death soon follows.

Each color has its own vibration and therefore its own healing abilities, which affect certain parts of the body and mind. Below is a list of the colors and a brief summary of each color's effects.

The following methods should not be used instead of a physician's care. These techniques are meant to augment the treatment you already receive from your health-care provider.

Here are the Colors and some of their basic meanings and uses for healing.

- **White** - White is a very cleansing color. Use white when you are not sure which color to employ.
- **Red** - Red stimulates anything in physical or mental form.. It invigorates the mind and creates deeper passions.
- **Orange** - Orange can be good at clearing out negativity in the mind.
- **Yellow** - Yellow is good for stimulating the mind. It inspires confidence and optimism.
- **Green** - Green has a calming effect on one's senses. Some claim that green helps people who suffer from exhaustion.
- Blue   Blue is a good cooling color.
- **Indigo** - Indigo, according to some Wiccans, balances the brain. They suggest that it supports one's immune system.
- **Violet** - Violet helps balance the body and the mind. Some Wiccans suggest that it heals the brain by inducing the sleep state for dreams.

As you can see from above, many ailments can be treated with color.

Light Therapy

You can use colored light, preferably sunlight and colored glass. The purity of color is important. Place the colored glass against the glass of a window so that the sun passes through it and creates a colored beam. Next, sit and place the ailing area of your body within the beam.

You can use colored light bulbs for similar healing. You can arrange electric lights to treat multiple areas at the same time.

Whether you use the sun or colored light bulbs, practice deep breathing. Visualize taking in the colored light on your in-breath. Upon exhaling, imagine breathing out your affliction.

An important part of healing is changing your vibrational state. If you choose to augment your healing process with Light Therapy, still recall that the best method of changing your vibrational state is by using music, singing and chanting. That's why Wiccans do those activities.

Wearing Colors for Healing

When you choose to wear certain colors, you will be using the subtractive system of color (mentioned above). Have you wondered why people have favorite colors and wear certain colors more often than others? The colors that one favors are usually colors that we need to absorb in our aura. People have been using color for self-medicating purposes for thousands of years. Many just didn't realize it at the time.

So if you have a medical condition, consider supplementing your physician's care by wearing an appropriate healing color. Again look at the *second* color chart to identify a helpful color.

Amulets and Talismans

A number of people confuse amulets and talismans with each other. Amulets are found objects that are not altered. Talismans are man-made in some way, by cutting or shaping or forging. They are both used for the same thing, to hold a charge for magic.

Talisman: A talisman is a charged occult object that attracts something specific to the person. Talismans are usually metal, like coins that are inscribed with symbols and a great deal of work goes into shaping them. Some talismans are made of parchment with symbols inked into them. Wiccans wear certain talismans and place other ones in secret, safe places. What do people often use talismans for? To attract love, good luck, fame, wealth, or other positive experiences.

For example, I always wear a pentacle necklace, and I feel that it does two positive things: it keeps me safe, and simultaneously it repels negative entities. You might ask, "What negative entities?" According to Wiccan beliefs, there are mischievous entities who like to disrupt some people's lives. Wearing my talisman brings me peace of mind.

Wiccans have discovered that natural objects hold a charge better than certain items like plastic, polyester, and so forth.

Talismans can be made of wood, stone, metal, or any other natural material, even parchment. These materials can then be inscribed with words, numbers and other symbols.

A prime requirement for a talisman is that it be made of a material that can hold a magickal charge.

Charging means putting your energy into something, such as a talisman.

Since natural substances are best at holding a "charge," make your talisman by hand and then charge it with a specific purpose. From that point forward, the talisman will act on your behalf. You can wear your talisman or place it in a safe place where it will not be disturbed.

I recommend that you consider keeping a diary about the results you are getting with your talisman. Usually, talismans retain their charge for a couple of months. Some Wiccans recharge their talisman every six months, but this all depends on how adept the person is in charging the talisman in the first place. The point of keeping your diary, which is really a part of your *Book of Shadows,* is to observe how your magickal efforts are yielding results you desire.

A Book of Shadows (BOS) can be a binder or even a file on a computer that consists of everything from spells to rituals and more. Some people like to keep their magickal diary separate from their BOS, but I feel it is just as appropriate to keep one section of your BOS for this purpose. It's up to you.

Amulet: Amulets are always found in nature: wood, stone, metal in its natural state, and crystals. Since amulets are natural objects, they are charged naturally, meaning they hold energy already.

Amulets, unlike talismans, tend to be used for broader purposes instead of a specific purpose. Amulets work in a passive way working on what comes into the wearer's life.

Wiccans use an amulet to ward off misfortune or danger. For example, a four-leaf clover can be used as symbol to bring protection into your life. It is said to ward off bad luck, and only lets good fortune find you. Wiccans wear amulets and sometimes place them in a purse or pocket. Many people hang them over their front door to keep their homes and the occupants safe.

Lucky Charms:

Lucky charms are not only *magickally delicious*, but they are also a talisman. (Yeah, it's a breakfast cereal pun.)

As a talisman, a lucky charm can be used to attract good luck.

On the other hand, they are *passive* like amulets in the sense that they wait for something to come your way before it does something for you.

When you form a lucky charm, remember the "an harm none" clause. We do not use animals or animal parts (unless they are shed naturally like feathers) in our rites. Using animals or animal parts is cruel, and that creates negative energy. Instead, you want to charge your lucky charms with positive energy.

Other Magick and Spells
Enchanting a silver ring for protection, prosperity and luck

This is a great way to bundle protection, prosperity and luck all in one. This is also one way to make a lucky charm.

What you will need:
- Your altar
- Your tools
- Silver Ring (925 or better is best)
- Your written script with the spell below

- A script to cast your circle
- Cakes and wine or juice for the ritual

To cast the ring spell:

1) Cast your circle.

2) Take the silver ring and asperge. Then cense (waft incense smoke around) the silver ring.

3) Hold up the silver ring and say:

Little trinket ring of mine,
Listen up, for it is time.
Let my little circle of silver grow,
Bring me great success and luck for me to know.

And give me great protection from all baneful powers of the hour,
Only protection, success and good luck, I do ask for it to shower.

And I never forget to state this line,
Protect me from all danger and sorrow so I'll be just fine.

All this I do ask plus one more thing,
And it harm none, not one thing!

4) Place ring down on pentacle and point the tip of your wand to the ring and say:

Great Lord and gracious Lady, I call you now,
Instill your power in this, my ring, right now.

I ask for your fertility of abundance, luck and
protection,

Blessed be this ring with your perfection.
So mote it be!

10) After the spell is finished, do the cakes and wine/juice ritual.

11) Close your circle.

* * * * * *

Magick Herbs

Wiccans use herbs for all sorts of things from medicine to protection. Humans have used herbal remedies made from plants for thousands of years. Herbs comprise the oldest medicines humans have had. Many Wiccans use herbs to heal and keep themselves healthy. Being witches, we want to use nature as our healer when we get sick.

Before considering the use of herbs, heed these important considerations:

1) If you have a serious condition and/or illness, modern medicine should be used in conjunction with the old ways. For example, you shouldn't skip a trip to a medical doctor because you have heard that St. John's Wort would help with depression. Always consult with your medical doctor about herbs you're considering because some herbs may conflict with medications your doctor has prescribed or over

the counter medications—or even other herbs.

2) Avoid taking an herb that you are unfamiliar with. Some herbs can be quite dangerous if used incorrectly. Certain herbs are poisonous like Belladonna. So always talk with your herbal-friendly medical doctor before taking them.

3) Some herbs you may buy at a New Age store may only be graded for magickal use. This means do NOT take such herbs internally. Be certain that the herbs you buy are food grade safe. Just because feverfew tea helps reduce a fever does NOT mean that you shouldn't use aspirin or some other modern medicine if the fever is really bad and doesn't go down. Be smart and use your head. If your affliction is serious, consult a medical doctor.

You will notice that each herb has an element, a ruling planet, and a gender. I know that the "Sun" and the "Moon" are scientifically not planets, but our ancestors didn't realize this, and so I will use the term "planet" to refer to heavenly bodies in general. The gender describes attributes the plant exhibits. Some of the male attributes are lust, sexual potency strength, and any of the more fiery properties. Some feminine properties are love, beauty, healing, and psychic powers.

The Herbs

Warning: People can discover that they are allergic to herbs that they've never used before. Be careful.

Allspice

Element: Fire
Planet: Mars
Gender: Masculine

Magickal Uses: Allspice can be easily obtained from most supermarkets or spice stores. It is a brownish powder and has a nice aromatic smell. It can be burned as an incense to attract money or luck.

Healing Uses: This herb can be used in ointments to help in healing. It can also be ingested for such purposes. Many people use it in baking today, so it is safe to ingest.

Aloe

Element: Water
Planet: The Moon
Gender: Feminine

Magickal Uses: It protects homes from accidents and protects you from evil energies.

Healing Uses: Aloe is a great healing plant, traditionally use to heal wounds. You can find this plant in many plant nurseries and stores. It has stubby green leaves with small spikes. To soothe burns, simply slice open the leaf and spread the juices on the burn site or wound area.

Apple

Element: Water
Planet: Venus
Gender: Feminine

Magickal Uses: The apple is a great choice for drawing love to you. Use the blossoms in sachets for attracting love. The flowers can be used in incense and potions. As a side note: during Samhain, Wiccans decorate their altars with one or more apples.

Healing Uses: Remember the saying *an apple a day keeps the doctor away.* Eating apples helps keep you healthy. Apples help regulate the digestive system. The pectin in apples provides some relief from diarrhea. Apple's high fiber helps with constipation. The leaves of the apple tree contain phloretin which acts like a natural antibiotic.

Avocado

Element: Water
Planet: Venus
Gender: Feminine

Magickal Uses: The avocado functions as an aphrodisiac. It is said that carrying an avocado pit will enhance your beauty.

Healing Uses: Research suggests that eating avocado as part of a salad allows one's body to more readily absorb fat-soluble nutrients. For example, one 2005 study demonstrated that eating avocado helped research subjects to absorb three to five times more carotenoids (antioxidant molecules). Such antioxidant molecules assist one's body to avoid free radical damage. (A "free radical" is an atom or group of atoms that has at least one unpaired electron. Such free radicals can cause damage related to cancer.)

Banana

Element: Water
Planet: Venus
Gender: Feminine

Magickal Uses: The banana is a fertility plant. It is used to cure impotency and create fertility. All parts of the banana tree are used for prosperity spells.

Healing Uses: Bananas have a high iron content and therefore help form hemoglobin in the blood, which can help anemia. Due to bananas' high potassium content, eating this fruit can help with relieving muscle cramping.

Basil

Element: Fire
Planet: Mars
Gender: Masculine

Magickal Uses: Basil is easily found at supermarkets and can be used is sachets and incense. Wiccans use basil for attracting wealth and love. Carried in a sachet, this plant can also be used for protection from negative entities. I've used basil for creating a money-drawing oil. I've also used basil as a form of incense by burning the leaves on charcoal. I felt good vibrations while doing the associated rituals.

Healing Uses: Basil is safe to eat and can be used in teas and ointments. It helps in digestion and has anti-gas properties.

Blackberry

Element: Water
Planet: Venus
Gender: Feminine

Magickal Uses: This plant provides protection, healing, and prosperity. Blackberry bushes have thorns, and this detail inspires the Wiccan belief of blackberries as a form of protection. Wiccans also use blackberry leaves in spells to acquire money.

Healing Uses: Blackberries are high in antioxidants. A number of people report that blackberry leaves relieve diarrhea. I eat blackberries as part of a healthy shake that includes raspberries, blackberries, banana, spinach, and a cup of non-fat milk.

Boneset

Element: Water
Planet: Saturn
Gender: Feminine

Magickal Uses: Wiccans use boneset to drive away evil spirits. You can make an infusion out of it and sprinkle the mixture around your living area to drive the negative entities away.

Healing Uses: Wiccans use boneset for colds and flu. They make a tea and drink it. It is also used to treat arthritis because of its anti-inflammatory properties. I feel that drinking boneset tea has helped me heal my osteoporosis to an extent.

Buchu

Element: Water
Planet: The Moon
Gender: Feminine

Magickal Uses: Some Wiccans report using buchu (also known as Agathosma betulina) in an infusion/tea to induce psychic powers and prophetic dreams.

Healing Uses: It's reported that buchu can be used for urinary tract infections and as a diuretic to help with bloating during a woman's menstrual cycle.

Buckthorn

Element: Water
Planet: Saturn
Gender: Feminine

Magickal Uses: Some Wiccans report that buckthorn can be used for protection and granting wishes. Such individuals claim that buckthorn can help in legal matters when carried or worn to court. Buckthorn is an all-around good luck bringer.

Healing Uses: Some Wiccans speak of using this herb for relieving constipation. **However, be warned:** This herb is strong and may cause "the runs."

Catnip

Element: Water
Planet: Venus
Gender: Feminine

Magickal Uses: This herb is great for cat magick. When used in cat spells, catnip helps you and your cat bond. It can be used in beauty and friendship spells. Catnip attracts good spirits to you when you grow it near your home.

Healing Uses: This herb when used as an infusion/tea can help relieve indigestion and heartburn. Some Wiccans use catnip as a slight sedative for humans. It works great as a relaxing tea before bed.

Cedar

Element: Fire
Planet: The Sun
Gender: Masculine

Magickal Uses: Cedar when burned is an effective herb for purification. It is also a great choice in protection from evil.

Healing Uses: It is good at repelling pests, especially of the moth variety.

Celery

Element: Fire
Planet: Mercury
Gender: Masculine

Magickal Uses: Chewing the seeds is said to help with concentration. Wiccans also use celery seeds in dream pillows to promote sleep.

Healing Uses: Some Wiccans report that celery extract helps relieve gout. In Chinese medicine, celery is sometimes used to treat high blood pressure. It has been said that celery seeds reduce blood sugar levels, which would help diabetics.

Chamomile

Element: Water
Planet: The Sun
Gender: Masculine

Magickal Uses: Used to fight curses and spells. It is also a great herb to attract money.

Healing Uses: Wiccans use chamomile to support sleep. It's said to reduce anxiety and stress.

Cinnamon

Element: Fire
Planet: The Sun
Gender: Masculine

Magickal Uses: It is used for success, psychic powers, lust, and love spells. It can be burned as incense to attract money and to bring back health.

Healing Uses: Some research studies suggest that cinnamon helps in cases of high blood glucose levels.

Dill

Element: Fire
Planet: Mercury
Gender: Masculine

Magickal Uses: Dill can be used for protection when hung in the home or carried in a purse. Placing this herb over a doorway is said to block negative influences from entering. Because it has a large number of seeds, dill is often used in money and prosperity spells.

Healing Uses: Besides being a great preservative, dill helps in other ways. It helps the digestive tract by relaxing the muscles in your digestive system, and it also helps urinary tract infections. It does this by inhibiting the bacteria that cause bladder infections.

The Hidden Children of the Goddess

Dragon's Blood

Element: Fire
Planet: Mars
Gender: Masculine

Magickal Uses: Some Wiccans use dragon's blood for protection and exorcism. This is a great herb to use in incense to boost your spell's power.

Healing Uses: Some consider dragon's blood as a food preservative because of its high phenolic content. **Warning:** It is dangerous to use dragon's blood because merely getting the oil on one's skin causes bruising.

Eucalyptus

Element: Water
Planet: Moon
Gender: Feminine

Magickal Uses: Eucalyptus leaves and pods can be carried for protection. Wiccans sometimes stuff a healing poppet with eucalyptus leaves. (See the section following herbs for more information on poppets.)

Healing Uses: Eucalyptus loosens phlegm and helps you cough the goop up. It has antibacterial properties, and it helps heal minor scrapes and cuts.

Fennel

Element: Fire
Planet: Mercury
Gender: Masculine

Magickal Uses: Wiccans use fennel to ward off evil spirits. You can grow fennel in containers in various spots in the home. You may also hang fennel by windows and doors.

Healing Uses: Fennel is said to promote the production of bile. Either chewing the seeds or making a tea out of fennel helps the digestive tract.

Feverfew

Element: Water
Planet: Venus
Gender: Masculine

Magickal Uses: When carried, feverfew protects you from accidents, colds, and fevers.

Healing Uses: Some Wiccans consider feverfew tea to be great at reducing fevers.

Flax

Element: Fire
Planet: Mercury
Gender: Masculine

Magickal Uses: Flax is used to ward off poverty and to increase prosperity. You use it by placing some flax seeds in your purse or wallet.

Healing Uses: When eaten, flax can reduce cholesterol because it is high in fiber. Because of its high fiber content, flax can reduce blood sugar levels.

Frankincense

Element: Fire
Planet: The Sun
Gender: Masculine

Magickal Uses: Wiccans use frankincense for protection from evil and exorcising evil. Some Wiccans burn frankincense to induce visions to assist with their personal growth.

Healing Uses: A number of people use frankincense to promote healing and to prevent scarring left by wounds.

Garlic

Element: Fire
Planet: Mars
Gender: Masculine

Magickal Uses: Wiccans use garlic for healing and protection. A number of individuals use garlic as an anti-theft herb. It is said to keep "sticky fingers away."

Healing Uses: Garlic has antibacterial properties. For this reason, garlic is useful for some skin rashes.

Ginger

Element: Fire
Planet: Mars
Gender: Masculine

Magickal Uses: It is said that eating ginger before doing your magick spells helps increase your power. Ginger is often used in love spells too. Ginger root can be ground up and sprinkled in your pocket or purse/wallet to increase prosperity.

Healing Uses: This herb is used as a anti-nausea medicine for motion sickness and morning sickness.

Ginseng

Element: Fire
Planet: The Sun
Gender: Masculine

Magickal Uses: Wiccans use ginseng in love, beauty, protection, and lust spells. You can carry a ginseng root to attract love and also to guard your health.

Healing Uses: Ginseng is known for enhancing the immune system. **Warning:** It is reported that some people experience insomnia, menstrual problems, increased heart rate, high or low blood pressure, or other side effects.

Hibiscus

Element: Water
Planet: Venus
Gender: Feminine

Magickal Uses: Wiccans use the blossoms in love incenses for spells and in sachets.

Healing Uses: It is said that drinking hibiscus tea daily lowers high blood pressure. Researchers state that more studies are needed to verify this suggestion.

Hops

Element: Air
Planet: Mercury
Gender: Masculine

Magickal Uses: Wiccans include hop in protection charms. They sometimes scatter hops on a floor and use it during an exorcism ritual.

Healing Uses: It is controversial as to how hops serve for medicinal purposes. Some homeopathic practitioners suggest that hops serve to calm and relieve muscle spasms.

Juniper

Element: Fire
Planet: The Sun
Gender: Masculine

Magickal Uses: Some Wiccans use juniper for protection against evil forces, theft, accidents, and wild animal attacks.

Healing Uses: Some individuals use it in certain forms to help one breathe more freely. Some people find juniper similar to pepper for increasing circulation.

Lavender

Element: Air
Planet: Mercury
Gender: Masculine

Magickal Uses: Lavender is used in love sachets and for purification baths. Many use lavender as part of aroma therapy in that it promotes peace and happiness.

Healing Uses: Lavender can be used for reducing anxiety and stress. I have incorporated lavender in my personal, homemade hand balm. I find it calming. It helps me relax and sleep well. I have a friend who has used lavender oil for poison ivy. It helps relieve the itch and helps dry up the lesions. Its smell, though not unpleasant, is very intense, so she never used it at work, only at home.

Licorice

Element: Water
Planet: Venus
Gender: Feminine

Magickal Uses: Chewing on licorice (not the candy) can aid in love spells and is often used in sachets for such purposes.

Healing Uses: Some Wiccans use licorice as a cough remedy and for relieving sore throats.

Myrrh

Element: Water
Planet: The Moon
Gender: Feminine

Magickal Uses: Wiccans burn myrrh to purify an area. Myrrh helps boost the power of other incenses, and it is often incorporated in the manufacture of a number of incense sticks.

Healing Uses: Myrrh fights bacteria. Ancient Egyptians used myrrh as a mouthwash.

Passion Flower

Element: Water
Planet: Venus
Gender: Feminine

Magickal Uses: When placed in the home, passion flower promotes peace. Passion flower in the bedroom makes it easier to fall asleep.

Healing Uses: Passion flower is used to combat stress, anxiety, and insomnia.

Pomegranate

Element: Fire
Planet: Mercury
Gender: Masculine

Magickal Uses: Eating the seeds helps increase fertility. Use the dried skin of the pomegranate in money spells of all kinds.

Healing Uses: The pomegranate has excellent antioxidant properties.

Raspberry

Element: Water
Planet: Venus
Gender: Feminine

Magickal Uses: Ancient peoples considered raspberry to be good for protection because it has thorns. The fruit is great for love spells and potions.

Healing Uses: Some Wiccans use raspberry fruit as a tea for relieving diarrhea.

St. John's Wort

Element: Fire
Planet: The Sun
Gender: Masculine

Magickal Uses: Place St. John's Wort in a container and hang it by window for protection.

Healing Uses: A number of people report that St. John's Wort has helped relieve them from depressed feelings. It is said that St. John's Wort helps in treating seasonal affective disorder, which is depression caused by a lack of sunlight in the winter months. **Warning:** *Talk with medical professionals about using St. John's Wort whether in place of or with standard anti-depression western medicines. Also, be careful about mixing St. John's Wort with other medicinal remedies.*

Valerian

Element: Water
Planet: Venus
Gender: Feminine

Magickal Uses: A number of Wiccans use valerian in love sachets and for protecting their home.

Healing Uses: Some Wiccans use valerian as a remedy for insomnia. Valerian root is the active agent in Valium, a medical sedative, so it should *not* be used as a tea by people taking that medication. They can overdose.

* * * * * *

The Sachet

First, we're going to discuss a container for herbs known as a sachet. Take a small piece of cloth in a color that corresponds with the type of magick you will be doing. See this color chart below:

- Red: sex, desire, vitality, strength.
- Orange: charm, confidence, joy, jealousy, persuasion.
- Yellow: intellectual development, joy, intellectual strength.
- Green: prosperity, abundance, fertility, money matters.
- Blue: healing, protection, spiritual development.
- Purple: the occult, power, magick.
- Pink: love, friendship, compassion.
- Black: decrease, death, revenge, retribution, contacting the dead. (I strongly suggest that you take great care if you have any thoughts about revenge or retribution. The focus points of revenge or retribution hurt the practitioner! Remember the Law of Three! I strongly recommend avoiding the use of black cloth except for the Samhain practice of contacting the dead.)

Place the piece of cloth down onto the table or working surface. Place selected herbs (about a tablespoon when all combined) in the middle of your cloth. You can use a smaller amount for a smaller more portable sachet if you like. This can be placed in your purse or pocket to be carried with you. Gather up your corners of the cloth and then tie them with some string. Make the sachet closed and secure. Now you can do a ritual to dedicate the sachet to its purpose.

Poppets

What is a poppet? A poppet is a doll made of cloth and stuffed with herbs. Wiccans often make a poppet to represent themselves.

Poppets are easy to make. Take two rectangular pieces of cloth. Draw a human shape (like a ginger bread man) on one piece of your fabric. Lay one piece on top of the other and cut out the shape. You should have two cut out pieces of cloth that are the same shape and size. Next start with the body and sew up both sides together, sewing everything but the head; leave that open.

You'll need to decide which herbs will best suit your desires. For example, you might use cinnamon (yes, I know it is a spice) to attract money. Or you might choose rose petals to attract love and friendship.

Take your herbs and your poppet. Once you have filled the body, sew up the head to seal the herbs inside. You can add hair or other features to your doll to make it look more like you.

Hold your completed poppet in your hands and visualize your intent. You can chant to help charge your poppet.

When you are done, place the poppet in a safe place where it will not be disturbed until you need to use it again.

Now that you have your poppet, what's next? You need to connect your poppet so that what you do for healing to the doll takes effect in you. This simple ritual below will help you to do this. (A basic version of this ritual was found in the Australian magazine Witchcraft. I have modified it for my purposes here.)

1) Cast your circle in the usual way (see Casting Circle in Chapter 12.)

2) Place the poppet on altar pentacle. Place your hands over or on the poppet and say:

Little one, I made you and now I give you life
I name you (your name)
Your body is my body
Your breath is my breath
Your passion is my passion
Your blood is my blood
Though separate we were
Now we are one.

3) Do the Cakes and Wine ritual.

4) Close the Circle.

Once you have done this, you can use your poppet in spell work.

Poppet Wealth Spell

The oldest poppet spells were for healing parts of the body and the acupuncture meridian dolls are one form of this. The Venus of Wallendorf is the oldest representative of a poppet, used for fertility and sex magic.

So why are we exploring the use of a Poppet Wealth Spell? To say it plainly, I've met a significant number of people who need healing in their financial abundance area of life.

A wealth spell is not only about money in and of itself. It's about abundance for food, rent and even gifts for loved ones. Of course we live in a society that uses money to exchange for goods. Think of it: "goods." So let's welcome abundance with an appropriate use of magick.

Assemble these items:
- Your ritual tools
- Poppet of you

- Coin
- Green string
- Cakes and Wine

1) Cast your circle in the usual way (see Casting Circle in Chapter 12).

2) Hold your poppet in your hands and visualize your intent. Use one of the energy raising techniques from Chapter 11, like chanting, to help charge your poppet with your intent. Visualize money flowing to you. See your wealth building up. See all the things that you can do with the money. While saying this spell, use the green string to tie the coin to the poppet.

3) Now holding the poppet say:

Lovely Lady of the Moon,
Bring to me wealth right soon.
Lovely Lady be my guide,
Open up your bounty wide.
Fill my hands with silver and gold.
All you give me, my hands can hold.
Lovely lady let there be no hitches,
No fear or woes with these riches.
So Mote it be!

4) Do the Cakes and Wine ritual.

5) Close the circle.

Place your poppet in a safe place after its use, a place where it will not be disturbed or discovered.

Another variation of this poppet wealth spell can include filling your poppet with herbs related to prosperity. Place the poppet on your altar and visualize money coming to the poppet. You might also tie some paper money to your poppet.

You can use poppets for a variety of purposes, but Wiccans most often use poppets for healing.

When you are done, place the poppet in a safe place where it will not be disturbed until you use the poppet again.

Infusion/Brew or Potion

What is an infusion or potion? They're the result of soaking herbs in hot water to bring out their properties. Human beings have healed themselves through herbs since prehistoric times. I suggest the book, The New Healing Herbs: The Essential Guide to More Than 125 of Nature's Most Potent Herbal Remedies by Michael Castleman.

Warning: *Only use herbs that you are certain to be food grade. In addition, always talk to your doctor before using any herb. Herbs by themselves can cause harmful effects. For example, chamomile can cause uterine contractions, which may lead to miscarriage, so pregnant women are advised to avoid chamomile.*

Furthermore, herbs can mix with each other or with medications in harmful ways. You need accurate information before you ingest any herbs. Find credible professionals who have expertise with alternative medicine because a number of western medicine doctors do not have great knowledge in this area.

The simplest example of an infusion, brew, or potion is tea. We drink teas, but not all potions or brews are meant to be ingested.

Second warning: *Never make a potion with poisonous plants!*

After you have done some research and consulted a doctor and have chosen a safe herb, you can make a tea. Heat water to almost a boil and add selected herbs into a ceramic container, like a cup.

Pour the water over herbs and place a cover over the container to steep the brew. The cover keeps most of the steam in, and this helps keep the essential oils in your potion. Then let the portion steep for about 5 to 10 minutes. Strain the mixture. We have been talking about tea; however, you can use brews for other uses. For example, you can use brews to cleanse spaces by asperging areas or by washing the floors and other surfaces with them. You may anoint things like sachets, talismans, and amulets. Herbs may be used for a ritual bath. Once again, be sure the plants are safe for their intended use.

You can also use the sun to make potions. Take a clear jar and fill it with water and your herb mixture. Place the jar in direct sunlight for six hours or so and then use.

You can use potions . . .

• for drinking in a tea (when appropriate)
• to wash your floors or wipe furniture.
• to augment your bath water for when you rest and soak.

Herbs as Ointments

When I make an ointment using herbs, I use vegetable shortening. You can use lard if you want, but this substance smells terrible.

To make an herb ointment, use one cup of vegetable shortening to three tablespoons herbs.

Melt shortening down, add herbs into the base, and let it steep for 5 to 10 minutes. Strain the liquid and let it cool. Store sealed, air tight, in a cool place. That's how we make an herb ointment. Be sure to use a glass jar or ceramic jug to store it in. Using plastic or metal will interfere with the ointment's chemistry. For example, plastic has chemicals that can leach out in your ointment.

Where do you apply it?

Depending on what you're using it for, apply to affected area (perhaps a rash that needs healing) or dab on wrists and neck. Never put an ointment on an open wound, however. This will block off air flow to the wound and can cause infection.

Ointments can often smell nice (like my lavender ointment), and that's a great two-for-one opportunity: healing and a pleasant fragrance.

Magick Oils

You can choose from an assortment of different oils to use in magick. Wiccans use oils to anoint candles, sachets, talismans, amulets, crystals, and people. Consider using oils for aromatherapy or mixing with other ingredients to make incense or ointments. You can also wear oils like perfumes.

An oil's scent creates energy, which we use in our magick.

Make sure that the oils you use are genuine and authentic essential oils—in other words, that they are made from the plants themselves. The plant's oils carry the plant's properties and energies that we use in our magick. Many distributors will slap on the label "essential oil" to make a buck, but many of these are synthetic scents, which do not carry a plant's vital energies or properties. For this you need genuine oils that come directly from the plant itself.

Undiluted oils can irritate your skin. So dilute them by adding them to a base oil. To do this, take 1/8 cup of a base oil such as Jojoba oil. Then, using an eye dropper, place around 6 drops of the undiluted essential oil into your base oil. Swirl in a clockwise direction to mix. Then you can use this mixture on the skin for anointing.

To anoint the body, rub your diluted oil mixture on your wrists, neck, and sometimes behind the knees if desired. This will let your body absorb the energies of the oils.

In Conclusion

There are many ways to do magick. You will get results whether you use candle magick, color magick, an amulet or talisman, or just your mind.

Chapter Questions

1. Is it okay to practice magick with a previously owned tool?
2. What is the difference between an amulet and talisman?
3. Name two different ways to do color healing.

CHAPTER 14:
DIVINATION & THE TAROT

Divination is a method of finding out information that we are not normally privy to. For example, people use it to learn about the future. People also use divination to find lost objects and even to locate water under the ground.

The Tarot

Wiccans use the Tarot as a useful divinatory tool. Learning it takes practice, practice, and more practice. I have found that the best way to learn the meaning of each card is to throw away the instruction book. Calm down, calm down ... Take a breather ... Okay.

Tarot cards come with instruction books that explain each card and its meaning. If you would like someone else's opinion, then please read the book. However, it is my contention that what the cards mean to you is certainly more important than what they mean to someone else. This chapter will help you discover your own definitions.

Tarot uses your intuition and subconscious mind to listen

to the "universal pipeline" to find the answers you seek. With practice, you can interpret each card by the graphic it contains and when and where it shows up as it is used. The positions and the meanings for those positions will help you. In this way you can decipher the answers to your questions. Sound simple? It can be. But only with practice will you learn to "read" what the cards are saying.

In the beginning:

The what, where, when, and who

We know that playing cards were invented in China around the 9th century. We know less, about how the Tarot came to be. Thanks to the research of Stuart Kaplan, Thierry Depaulis, Ronald Decker, and Michael Dummett, most people in the Tarot community agree that Tarot cards originated from the mid to late 1400s.

The playing cards we know today migrated from the East (probably Egypt) to Europe around 1360. They were very popular, although the trumps did not yet exist. By 1377, widespread use of the cards was reported throughout Europe. It was these cards that slowly morphed into Tarot cards. The first Tarot decks, known as Trionfi and later as Tarocchi, are attributed to northern Italians around 1410 to 1425. However, we still do not know how many trumps (Numbered 0- 21 or Major Arcana) vs. just regular playing cards (everything else) were made at the time.

Thought of as one of the oldest remaining partial decks, the pictures of the cards are on a sheet in a book at The Library at Yale University. It's called the "Cary Sheet."

Since cards in the oldest decks were not numbered or titled, people relied on the imagery and oral tradition to tell them what the cards were and in which order they should be. It was the French who first set the ordering system of the trumps (Major Arcana) by affixing numbers to the cards.

The only existing record of this order of the cards comes from a sermon around 1500 that condemned card playing. Finally, French card-maker Catelin Geofroy published the first fixed-order deck in 1557.

Tarot continued moving along its journey toward becoming the cards that we know today. The cards were used for centuries as both playing cards as well as a divination tool. The rules for the modern game of Tarot (also called Tarocchi) were published in 1637. But it wasn't until the 18th century that people started using Tarot to tell the future.

What Suits You

Depending on which deck you use, the suits may be called by different names and represent different elements. Do not worry: we will discuss more about elements in a bit. I will use the Robin Wood Tarot Deck for this discussion. Many people prefer the Rider-Waite Tarot Deck. But I'm different. I find the Robin Wood deck to have a more pagan look, and I prefer its symbolism. But you can use whichever deck you choose.

In the Tarot, 78 cards are separated into two groups: the Major Arcana and the Minor Arcana. The Major Arcana has 22 cards. The rest are called the Minor Arcana. The Minor Arcana are divided into four groups: Pentacles (or Coins depending on the deck), Swords, Wands (or Staffs), and Cups. Each suit has cards ranking from the Ace (one) to the King just like a regular deck of cards.

Just like the four directions, each suit represents an element and a specific period in the life cycle. The list below indicates the basic meanings of each suit, including the season and time of day that each represents. When you do readings, you can add your own personal meanings to each suit. You will find that each card contains details that help you flesh out more meaning.

Let's look at the different suits and what they generally mean.

Pentacles (Coins)

- **Element:** Earth
- **Season of year:** Winter
- **Time of Day:** Midnight
- **Direction:** North

Pentacles are a girl's best friend! Pentacles, or coins as they are more commonly known, represent the mundane world (physical world)—and it's all about stuff! Pentacles are best known for their representation of money, but they can also stand for stillness.

Swords

- **Element:** Air
- **Season of year:** Spring
- **Time of Day:** Morning
- **Direction:** East

Swords are action! They symbolize logic and reasoning (not necessarily wisdom). They can be a symbol of strife or aggressive behavior. Swords can "cut" two ways, constructively or destructively.

Wands (Staffs)

- **Element:** Fire
- **Season of year:** Summer
- **Time of Day:** Noon
- **Direction:** South

Wands are the spark of intuition. They stand for focus, will, and growth. Their phallic image symbolizes the life force. They represent enthusiasm for life. The Wand also denotes authority (the one who holds the wand has power) and nimble speech.

Cups

- **Element:** Water
- **Season of year:** Fall
- **Time of Day:** Evening
- **Direction:** West

Cups are the emotional side of the Tarot. This includes all that comes from the heart, like love and friendship. Cups are the artistic side and also represent the subconscious.

It's All About the Numbers
This section discusses the meaning of the numbers on the Tarot cards. We will also delve a bit into numerology.

Cards Ace (One) through King
Each Tarot card has a defined meaning, and each meaning relates to the suit it is in:

- Ace: represents the meaning of the suit it is in and magnifies the lesson
  - Two: balance, tension, or equilibrium of the suit the card is in
  - Three: your spiritual path, mastery
  - Four: for change, going through activity to rest and/or joy to discontentment
  - Five: the negative side or attributes of the suit
  - Six: lessons learned and actions taken
  - Seven: decisions, facing a choice
  - Eight: a difficult challenge
  - Nine: a revelation
  - Ten: the logical conclusion
  - Page/Jack: the learning principle of the suit the card is in / what you can learn
  - Knight: the active principle of the suit the card is in / enforces rules
  - Queen: the reflective principle, a nurturing role; the queen guides you
  - King: the ruling principle; the king has a dominant role, he makes the rules

Additionally the face cards of the Tarot can represent people in your life.

Timing and Numbers

Each card represents a specific number of days, weeks, or months that something will happen. The card's number is read together with its suit. (See below.)

- Cards Ace through Ten: 1 through 10 days, weeks, or months. For instance, a 5 of Swords means something will happen in about 5 days. An Ace of Pentacles means something will happen in about

one month to one year.
- Page/Jack: 11 days, 11 weeks, or 11 months.
- Queen and King: unknown time (you're the factor for the time)

Suits and Timing
Each suit represents a different timeframe.
- Swords: days (something will happen fast)
- Wands: days to weeks
- Cups: weeks to months
- Pentacles: months to years (something will happen slowly)

Numerology and How to Find the Theme of Your Year
The following equation will determine your theme for the current year. To provide an example, I will use a sample birth date.

Month: 09
Day: 08
Current year: 2013
Now add together each number:
9 + 8 + 2013 = 2030
Now add together each number in the total:
2 + 0 + 3 + 0 = 5
Use the numbers on the Major Arcana to get your theme for the current year. You'll notice that for example, the theme is the Hierophant. A hierophant is someone who interprets sacred mysteries or arcane knowledge. So in this situation, one possible interpretation of the theme for the year is: One may face mysterious or religious challenges or changes.

0. The Fool
1. The Magician
2. The High Priestess
3. The Empress
4. The Emperor
5. The Hierophant
6. The Lovers
7. The Chariot
8. Strength
9. The Hermit
10. Wheel of Fortune
11. Justice
12. The Hanged Man
13. Death
14. Temperance
15. The Devil
16. The Tower
17. The Star
18. The Moon
19. The Sun
20. Judgment
21. The World

A similar formula will show your life path. Many Wiccans look upon the life path as the journey and goal of your time on this planet.

This time, use your birth date. Use the same list above to get your theme, that is, the central theme of your life path. For example "Kim's" birthday is September 7, 1993.

Month: 09
Day: 07
Birth year: 1993

Now add together each number:

$9 + 7 + 1993 = 2009$

Now add together each number in the total:

$2 + 0 + 0 + 9 = 11$

Kim's life path is Justice. One possible interpretation of this life path is that she may face a situation dealing with legal matters in her lifetime.

Spreadin' the Love
Examples of Some Tarot Spreads

A spread is how you place the Tarot cards on the table. Different spreads have different meanings. Select the spread based on what you want to learn.

The first and most popular spread is the Celtic Cross, which is shown here. It is preferred for its simplicity and the amount of information it provides. Most people use the Celtic Cross when they first begin reading cards.

The numbers indicate the order the cards are put on the table. Place each card face up in sequence. Determine its meaning before you proceed to the next card.

Reading Cards

Sometimes I have found that the cards can be astonishingly accurate if you can read them right. A lot of times you read something that does not make sense at that moment, but later it becomes clear. Think of one session of reading cards as a glimpse of strands of possibilities that are leading toward a particular future—at the moment you're reading the cards. Just because something is in the cards does not mean that it will automatically come true. Just by reading the cards you are affecting the strands of possibilities. That's why it's useful to have multiple readings.

I recall relating a detail for a particular client. He wanted to know if his business and a particular product were going to be successful soon. The cards indicated that things looked dim. However, just learning that things were not on an automatic track to success gave my client the juice to change details. A later reading showed that things looked more hopeful for his business's successful future.

You can use different processes to read the cards. When you start reading for the first time in the day or evening, tap on the deck three times. This tells the cards to wake up and that there is work to be done. This also knocks out or pushes out any bad energy or kinks of energy there are in the cards.

If you are reading for yourself, now think of the questions you want answered. Make the questions simple. Yes/no questions are good for this.

Once you have your question, it's time to pick out the "significator," a card which represents what the question is based on. If it is a question about your home, pick a card you feel represents your home. This will be the first card you place down.

From this point, I'll describe how you do a reading for someone else. *(Please note: For simplicity's sake, I'm using only feminine pronouns to refer to the person you are reading for. That him/her...his/her stuff gets old fast.)*

Ask the person to tell you her question and invite her to pick out a significator card and hand it to you. Next have the person shuffle the deck while holding her question in her mind.

Then spread the cards out and have the person pick out

ten cards. Place the cards as seen in the picture below.

Celtic Cross Spread

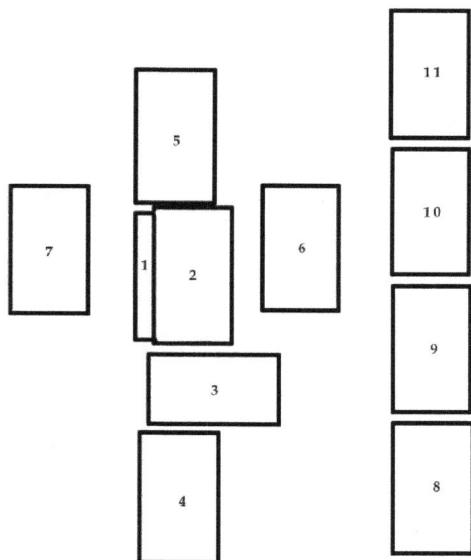

Card Definitions Following the Number Noted in the Graphic

- Card One: The Significator. This card represents the question being asked.
- Card Two: This card "covers the person." Covers means what is protecting or helping the person asking the question. This is the first of two opposing forces at work with the question.
- Card Three: This card "crosses the person." Crosses means what is blocking the person asking the question. This is not necessarily bad. For example, if a person is an addict and she is spiraling downward, her concerned parents may

be "crossing" or blocking her path of destruction. So Card Three is the second of the opposing forces at work with the question.

- Card Four: This card represents the foundation the person has pertaining to the question. This explains what the question or matter is built on.
- Card Five: This card identifies what the person was heading toward at the moment the question was asked.
- Card Six: The near past of the question.
- Card Seven: The near future of the question.
- Card Eight: The Tarot's answer to the question asked.
- Card Nine: The environment that surrounds the person pertaining to the question being asked.
- Card Ten: The hopes and fears of the person asking the question.
- Card Eleven: The final outcome for the person.

The Decision Spread

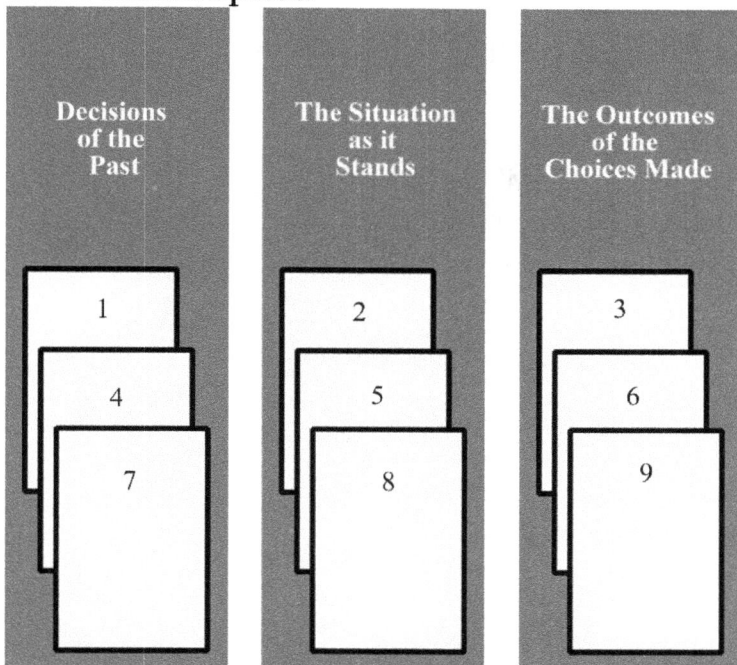

Decisions of the Past	The Situation as it Stands	The Outcomes of the Choices Made
1	2	3
4	5	6
7	8	9

Use the Decision Spread when hard decisions must be made. It helps you determine the correct decisions in a given situation. This spread has three columns with three cards in each. The first column analyzes your past decisions that created the situation. The second column examines the present moment. The third column shows the outcome of your choices.

In Conclusion

This chapter provided you with an introductory course on reading the Tarot. I hope you found it interesting and helpful.

You learned the importance of going with your own intuition. We covered the numbering system on each card and what the numbers generally mean. We explored some history of the Tarot and some basic numerology, and we covered some spreads that are used.

Chapter Questions
1. What is a "spread" in Tarot?
2. What is divination used for?
3. Why are numbers on the cards important in Tarot?

CONCLUSION

So why do all this? Why do we practice Wicca? Many just focus on the magick, and they concentrate on doing spells with the all the occult fixings such as candles, tools, incense, music, and more. They master the Tarot Cards and learn of the herbs and their lore.

Imagine you've studied long hours to understand the how of Wicca. And someone asks you why. What would you say?

When we wrap our heads around all the technicalities of the how, we sometimes miss the why. Yes, there is magick. Yes, you can make real change in the world around and within you. With all this work many still miss the whole reason for practicing at all. Why practice any faith for that matter?

The reason? It all comes down to connection with Deity. We yearn for that connection; no, we hunger for it. In all reality we need it to be whole. Many of us search high and low for it our whole lives, whether or not we acknowledge it. That drive surrounds us and can define who we are. The Craft can and does show us the path to our desires. We must look deep enough to find the secret for your personal path.

We use all these techniques to come closer to the All. Our path is a circle, as we ever continue to look for the All, in this incarnation and in others. The Craft holds the secret to what we most desire, if we dare to listen.

Looking back on my own journey I have seen myself grow in unexpected leaps and bounds. Starting from a shriveled, unnurtured seed, finding my way to the fertile soil that is Wicca and taking root there. With the nourishment of the Gods' and Goddesses' love I grew strong and became healthy.

I saw myself become the bud, with all the potential of the rose within. Finding the light of self love and respect within I bloomed and became the rose. As the rose I now experience abundance. With Wicca, I became a rose in a beautiful garden of my own making.

Use the tools of grounding, meditation, and the wisdom of the Gods in magick.

If you have questions or comments I would love to hear from you. Contact me at Askawitchnow@gmail.com

Blessed Be.

- Moonwater SilverClaw

AFTERWORD
BY ANGUS MCMAHAN

Does the world need another Wicca 101 book? Yes. The world needs this one.

Moonwater SilverClaw was inspired to write this, her first book, by the Gods themselves, but there is no high-flown rhetoric or elaborately constructed sentences chock-full of Scrabble words to be found here. *The Hidden Children of the Goddess* is rather more like sharing a nice cup of coffee with a new friend, while you two are taking a walk in the woods.

For this is not simply a laundry list of spells, colors and herbs - although all that is in here too! What *The Hidden Children of the Goddess* is really about is Moonwater SilverClaw's own personal journey, from childhood abuse, to depression, suicide attempts, crippling shyness and overcoming acute dyslexia to write first a weekly series of blog posts about Wicca and then, eventually, this wonderfully-wise little volume.

Her personal story is mixed in effortlessly in with the information on Sabbats and circle casting, Craft history and coven politics, altar items and divination techniques. In short, Moonwater has pulled off the very rare feat of making a Wicca 101 book that is both encyclopedic in knowledge AND conversational in tone.

I have followed the progress of this book as it appeared, serial fashion, in a series of weekly blog posts. Early on Miss SilverClaw reached out to me for some editing help and a few questions on Magickal practices and I was more than happy to share some info and give some encouragement. And I watched a hesitant writer work and work and work some more and gain some confidence and get a slew of positive comments and then reach her stride as a writer, speaker and High Priestess. But with *The Hidden Children of the Goddess* Moonwater SilverClaw has attained the rarest of prizes for us word-jockeys: She has found her Voice.

And that voice has a LOT to teach all of us, from the young person who wants to know why she feels 'special', to us seasoned practitioners of Wicca who can always benefit from a straight-forward review of the basics.

But there is even more to this volume. Moonwater includes:

- a step-by-step guide of how to deal with the misinformation and intolerance that we witches encounter almost every day,

- a fun list of quick magickal pick-me-ups,

- a full relationship separation ritual,

- a recipe for lamb stew

- and a zippy history of the Craft that shows how the consequences of one stormy crossing of the English Channel lead directly to the Witch Hunting craze of the 14th-18th centuries, and the hatred that still resonates in the daily prejudice leveled at Witches and the Craft.

Along the way we also learn her insights and revelations on the process of writing this very book. And its all down with a stripped down style that makes the reading The Hidden Children of the Goddess feel like a great conversation with a new friend, who turns out to be your oldest friend of all.

By the end of The Hidden Children of the Goddess you will know a lot about Wicca, about Moonwater SilverClaw, and you will know a lot more about yourself.

Enjoy...

Blessed Be,

Angus McMahan

Angus writes a pagan advice column for the Patheos Portal at:

http://www.patheos.com/blogs/askangus/

and a general humor blog just for fun:

http://www.angus-land.com

ABOUT THE AUTHOR

Moonwater SilverClaw is a Wiccan High Priestess and member of the Covenant of the Goddess and the New Wiccan Church. She has trained people new to Wicca. As the author of five books, she shares her personal story, revealing how Wicca saved her life and helped her strengthen herself to secure her release from an abusive marriage.

Moonwater has been practicing Wicca since 1990, first as a solitary and then in a coven.

Moonwater posts at her blog,

GoddessHasYourBack.com

[with visitors from 173 countries]

On Quora.com, her posts have more than 10,100 views. She felt called to write the blog even though she is dyslexic. She works with a team of editors. She says, "I wish to educate those who don't understand what the Craft is about. Some people may not yet identify themselves as pagan, but they'd like more information."

Moonwater has addressed college students in Comparative Religion classes for over ten years. She leads workshops. She lives with her cat Magick and her sweetheart of many years; he is one of her editors. She enjoys knitting and photography.

Her work is endorsed by Wiccan notables including Patrick McCollum (receiver of the Mahatma Gandhi Award for the Advancement of Religious Pluralism).

Moonwater SilverClaw can be contacted at:

AskAWitchNow@gmail.com

Or at her blog:

GoddessHasYourBack.com

APPENDIX A:
READING LIST

Buckland, Ray. *Buckland's Complete Book of Witchcraft*, 2nd Edition. Llewellyn Publications, 2002.

Buckland, Ray. *Practical Color Magick*. Llewellyn Publications, 1999.

Castleman, Michael. *The New Healing Herbs, The Essential Guide To More Than 125 of Nature's Most Potent Herbal Remedies*. Rodale Inc 2009.

Cunningham, Scott. Wicca: *A Guide for the Solitary Practitioner*. Llewellyn Publications, 1989.

Cunningham, Scott. *Cunningham's Encyclopedia of Magical Herbs*, Expanded & Revised Edition. Llewellyn Publications; 1st edition (October 1985).

Ferrar, Janet and Stewart. *Eight Sabbats for Witches*, Revised Edition. Phoenix Publishing, WA, 1988.

Ferrar, Janet and Stewart. *The Witches' God: Lord of the Dance*. Phoenix Publishing, WA, 1989.

Ferrar, Janet and Stewart. *The Witches' Goddess: The Feminine Principle of Divinity*. Phoenix Publishing, WA, 1987.

Ferrar, Stewart. *What Witches Do*. Robert Hale, 2010.

Fitch, Ed. *A Grimoire of Shadows: Witchcraft, Paganism & Magick*. Llewellyn Publications, 1996.

Frazer, James George. *The Golden Bough: A Study in Magic and Religion*, A New Abridgement from the 2nd and 3rd Editions. Oxford University Press, USA, 2009.

Gardner, Gerald. *High Magic's Aid*. Aurinia Books, 2010.

Gardner, Gerald. *The Meaning of Witchcraft*. Red Wheel/Weiser, 2004.

Gardner, Gerald. *Witchcraft Today*. Citadel, 2004.

Giles, Cynthia. *The Tarot: History, Mystery, and Lore*.

Touchstone, 1994.

Graves, Robert. *The White Goddess: A Historical Grammar of Poetic Myth*, Amended and Enlarged Edition. Farrar, Straus and Giroux, 1966.

Leland, Charles G. *Aradia or The Gospel Of The Witches*. Kessinger Publishing LLC, 2010.

Lipp, Deborah. *The Way of Four: Create Elemental Balance in Your Life*. Llewellyn Publications, 2004.

Marcoux, Tom. *Darkest Secrets of Spiritual Seduction Masters: How to Protect Yourself, Boost Your Psychological Immune System and Strengthen Your Spirit*. Tom Marcoux Media, LLC, 2011.

McCoy, Edain. *Sabbats: A Witch's Approach to Living the Old Ways*. Llewellyn Publications, 2001.

Murray, Margaret Alice. *The God of the Witches*. NuVision Publications, 2009.

Neal, Carl. *The Magick Toolbox: The Ultimate Compendium for Choosing and Using Ritual Implements and Magickal Tools*. Samuel Weiser, 2004.

Russell, Jeffrey B. and Alexander, Brooks. *A History of Witchcraft: Sorcerers, Heretics & Pagans*, 2nd Edition. Thames & Hudson, 2007.

Starhawk. *The Spiral Dance: A Rebirth of the Ancient Religion of the Goddess: 20th Anniversary Edition*. HarperOne, 1999.

Sylvan, Dianne. *The Circle Within: Creating a Wiccan Spiritual Tradition*. Llewellyn Publications, 2003.

Tognetti, Arlene. *The Complete Idiot's Guide to Tarot*, 2nd Edition. ALPHA, 2003.

Tognetti, Arlene and Flynn, Carolyn. *The Complete Idiot's Guide to Tarot Spreads Illustrated*. ALPHA, 2006.

Valiente, Doreen. *An ABC of Witchcraft Past and Present*. *Phoenix Publishing*, WA, 1988.

Valiente, Doreen. *Natural Magic*. Robert Hale, 1999.

Valiente, Doreen. *Witchcraft for Tomorrow*. Robert Hale, 1993.

Wood, Robin. *Robin Wood Tarot: The Book*. Robin Wood Enterprises, 1998.

Wood, Robin. *When, Why ... If*. Robin Wood Enterprises, 1997.

APPENDIX B:
RECIPES

Recipes make everything better!

Lamb Stew with Red Sauce
By Kay Pannell

2 lbs. lamb meat cut into 1-1/2 inch cubes
2 lbs. onions (tiny boiling onions or large, quartered)
3 cloves garlic, peeled and sliced
¼ cup olive oil
1 cup tomato sauce (or 2 oz. can of tomato paste diluted in 1 cup hot water)
2 Tbsp. vinegar or ½ cup red wine (I use apple cider vinegar)
2 tsp. salt
1 Tbsp pickling spices
3 cups boiling water
Small cubes of red potatoes
Carrots, peeled and cut in small wheels
Celery, cut in bite sizes
Mushrooms, sliced

1.   Cube meat.

2.   Heat oil in large pot with cover.

3.   Sauté onions with garlic until translucent and add meat to brown.

4.   Add tomato sauce, boiling water, seasonings, and vinegar.

(I put the pickling spices into a tea ball. I also add the tomato sauce, water, and vinegar in one pot and use a frying pan to cook the onions and brown the meat before putting it in the stew pot. That way the spices and sauce are heating while the meat and onions are browning.)

5.   Cover and simmer on top burners over stove on low heat until the meat is tender and the sauce is thick, about 2 hours. Add fresh vegetables during last 45 minutes of cooking time.

6.   Check midway. If the meat is sticky, add 1cup water and reduce heat.

* * * * * *

Lamb Stew with White Sauce
By Kay Pannell

2 packets Knorr's Leek Soup Mix
2 tsp Olive Oil (to coat frying pan)
2 large cloves of garlic
1 small bunch of green onions
2 lbs. stewing lamb
1 lb. of red potatoes

1.   Cut up the lamb in small rectangles.

2.   Put two packets of Knorr's Leek Soup Mix, made according to instructions, into a large pot on the stove. Keep

stirring it.

3.	Next, to it in a deep frying pan, put in olive oil on medium heat. Slice up two large cloves of garlic and one small bunch of green onions, and put them in the frying pan to cook for about 5-7 minutes, just to take the bite out of them.

4.	Put lamb meat in frying pan to cook with garlic and onions. Brown meat on all sides. Cook just enough to tenderize the lamb so that it isn't tough.

5.	Put the lamb and onions into the soup and change to a low simmer.

6.	Cut up red potatoes into small rectangles and add to soup.

7.	Keep the pot on simmer until the potatoes are done. This dish can be refrigerated and re-heated several times, and it gets better with age.

* * * * * *

Moonwater's Fall Pumpkin Bread

Makes 2 loaves.

3 ½ cups all-purpose flour
2 tsp. baking soda
1 ½ tsp. salt
2 tsp. cinnamon
2 tsp. Allspice
2 tsp. nutmeg
3 cups sugar
4 eggs, beaten
2 cups of fresh pumpkin (16 ounces if using canned pumpkin)

2/3 cup water (only if pumpkin is canned)

1/2 cup water (only if pumpkin is fresh or frozen)

1 cup vegetable oil

1 cup chopped pecans

1. Preheat oven to 325 F.

2. Combine flour, soda, salt, cinnamon, nutmeg, and sugar in large mixing bowl. Add eggs, water, oil, and pumpkin. Stir until blended.

3. Add nuts. Mix well.

4. Pour into two 9x5" loaf pans.

5. Bake 1 hour 30 minutes.

6. Cool slightly and take out of pans to let cool on a rack. It's best if you wrap, refrigerate, and wait a day before you eat it. It keeps well in the refrigerator and can be frozen.

* * * * * *

Moonwater's Spring/Summer Lemon Bars

2 ¼ cups all-purpose flour

2/3 cup confectioners' sugar

2 cubes butter

3 lemons

5 eggs

1 ½ cups granulated sugar

1. Preheat oven to 350 F.

2. Coat jelly-roll pan with baking spray.

3. Combine:

2 cups of flour

2/3 cup confectioners' sugar

2 cubes butter (or 1 cup butter)

4.   Press mixture firmly and evenly into jelly-roll pan.

5.   Bake 18-20 minutes or until slightly browned.

6.   Combine:

Zest from the three lemons

Lemon juice from the three lemons

5 eggs

1 ½ cups of granulated sugar

¼ cup of flour

7.   Mix until smooth and then pour over cooled and prepared crust.

8.   Bake 20-22 minutes until center, when pressed, is firm.

9.   Cool on rack and sift confectioners' sugar on top.

10.   Cut into bars and serve.

* * * * * *

Real Key Lime Pie
By Kay Pannell

1/2 cup lime juice from Key Limes (Persian limes)

1 - 14 oz. can of sweetened condensed milk

5 egg yolks

1.   Preheat oven to 375 F.

2.   Combine ingredients in bowl, blend well, and pour into pre-made graham cracker crust 9   inch pie pan.

3.   Put in pie for 15 minutes.

4.   Cool pie. For best results, cool in refrigerator for several hours before eating.

5.   Add whipped cream for garnish

Bon appétit!

APPENDIX C:
END NOTES

Page 16
Doreen Valiente, (from her 1964 speech). "Eight words the Wiccan Rede fulfill, An it harm none, do what ye will."

Page 20
Jeffrey B. Russell and Brooks Alexander, *A History of Witchcraft: Sorcerers, Heretics & Pagans*, Second Edition, by (Thames & Hudson, 2007). "The ultimate origin the English word 'witch' is the Indo-European root *weik, which has to do with religion and magic. . . "

Page 24
Scott Cunningham, Wicca: *A Guide for the Solitary Practitioner* (Llewellyn Publications, 1989).

Page 35
American Council of Witches. ". . . in 1978, the U.S. Army incorporated the Thirteen Principles of Wiccan Belief into its official handbook used by Army chaplains."

Page 39
Covenant of the Goddess. Founded in 1975, the Covenant of the Goddess is one of the largest and oldest Wiccan religious organizations. Wicca . . . . "Wicca, or Witchcraft, is an earth religion—a re-linking (re-ligio) with the life-force of nature, both on this planet and in the stars and . . . "

Page 54
1487, *Malleus Maleficarum, or The Hammer of the Witches,* was written in 1487.

Page 66
Mahendranath Gupta, 1883. "A number of blind men came to an elephant. . . "

Page 145

Heinrich Cornelius Agrippa (1486-1535), wrote books on occult philosophy. "Unless a man be born a magician, and God have destined him even from his birth to the work, so that spirits . . ."

Page 149

Kelly McGonigal, Ph.D., *The Willpower Instinct: How Self-Control Works, Why It Matters, and What You Can Do To Get More of It.* Avery. (2011) "Willpower is about harnessing the three powers of I will, I won't and I want to help you . . ."

Page 160-161

Jason Miller, *Financial Sorcery: Magical Strategies to Create Real and Lasting Wealth*, New Page Books. (2012)

Also from Moonwater SilverClaw:

EXCERPT FROM
GODDESS HAS YOUR BACK
by Moonwater SilverClaw

CHAPTER 1:
GODDESS HAS YOUR BACK

Would you like your Wiccan path to lift up your self-esteem?

Would you simply like to feel better?

This book helps you actually feel your connection with the Goddess on a daily basis—even moment to moment.

As I mentioned in my first two books, *The Hidden Children of the Goddess* and *Beyond the Law of Attraction to Real Magick,* Wicca saved my life and empowered me to leave an abusive marriage.

As a High Priestess, I have supported friends, family, and colleagues in times of need. My blog TheHiddenChildrenoftheGoddess.com gives me a weekly opportunity to support website visitors from over 173 countries.

This book gives *us* the space and time to really explore magickal practices, rituals, meditations and experiences that you'll find comforting and uplifting.

My journey upon this path began with meeting the Gods. The Gods showed me the true path to self love and acceptance. Where I saw nothingness and unworthiness, they showed me abundance and a unique specialness that I had.

Now I will let you in on a secret. *You have your own unique specialness that no one else has.* It is yours, and yours alone. This new path is yours to discover and walk. Just like my own path, your path is a beautiful discovery simply waiting for you. Prepare to step forward on this new, wondrous, and beautiful path.

Let's take the next step.

Secret of How to Do Magick

When I first started doing magick it was really hit or miss, most often *mess.* My spell work was just not as effective as I wanted it to be. What was I doing wrong?

If you have wondered the same thing, you have probably done similar mistakes. For example, I'd do a money spell, but I'd just get new problems!

The real problem was, like many people, I just wanted a big payday. What I didn't know was that this is really the wrong way to approach a lack of money.

Many, if not most, spells written today are focused on the external opportunities or even requesting gifts from the Gods. Focusing on just the external can create new problems.

What if I could tell you a **Secret of how to do magick** — in a way where you avoid ethics issues about money?

I have mentored a number of people about this *Secret.* Now I will share with you this Secret.

A phrase from the poem by Doreen Valiente entitled *The Charge of the Goddess* tells us how to do magick well. But many of us, like my younger self, just don't see it. The line I'm talking about is: "…if that which thou seekest thou findest not within thee, thou wilt never find it without thee."

This line invites us to look within as we approach our magickal work.

Instead of focusing on how to get money from outside sources, focus within. How? Instead of asking for a handout from the universe, ask, **"How I can create more energy in myself to obtain my desire? How can I make myself open to more prosperity?"**

Let's get more specific. You have been laid off and need a new job pronto! Bills are pilling up fast.

Let's use a sigil for this purpose.

How to Make Your Own Personal Sigils

Imagine putting a magical intention into an object. Why would you do that? Wiccans do this because they want the object to hold power to help them realize a personal desire. For example, you may be job hunting and you want the power of the object—in this case, a sigil—to assist you to get the ideal job.

Making your own personal sigils is easy. Some time ago, author/artist Austin Osman Spare devised a method for creating sigils.

Since that time, a number of authors have discussed Austin Osman Spare's process of making sigils. One book I appreciate is Frater U. D.'s *Practical Sigil Magic: Creating Personal Symbols for Success.*

I have made a couple of my own additions to the process.

First, throughout history, witches made sigils out of virgin parchment. But that is quite expensive. Also if you're vegan and will not wear leather, you will want to use something else. Why? Parchment is typically made from sheep skin. So let's talk about a process devoid of parchment.

I use the heavier art paper, the kind that absorbs ink and which can be infused with different tinctures made with herbs. Watercolor paper is a nice choice, too.

What about inks? You could use one of the many magickal inks on the market. My favorite is Dragons Blood

Ink. But magickal inks can be expensive. So you can make your own out of a high grade ink such as Winsor Newton ink or India ink. To make it a magickal ink just add some essential oil to it, like myrrh. Mix and consecrate.

You can even use Sharpie pens as author Peter Paddon suggests. Just make sure to designate specific pens for only magickal work. They'll be part of your set of magickal tools.

You can use different colors for different desires. Here is a short list of colors and meanings that I include in my book *The Hidden Children of the Goddess:*

- Red: sex, desire, vitality, strength
- Orange: charm, confidence, joy, persuasion
- Yellow: intellectual development, joy, intellectual strength
- Green: prosperity, abundance, fertility, money matters
- Blue: healing, protection, spiritual development
- Purple: the occult, power, magick
- Pink: love, friendship, compassion
- White: purity, innocence, peace, tranquility

Write out your desire on a scratch piece of paper; you can use a single word or a phrase. Some examples are:

- I want an ideal job for me at this time
- Happiness
- I need a new house
- Success

We'll now use the word "Success" as our example. Cross off all of the repeat letters in Success. You end up with S, U, C, and E. (You want only one of each letter that appears in the word.) Next, scramble the letters, getting S, E, U, and C (for example).

Now comes the fun part: Combine the letters together in an image.

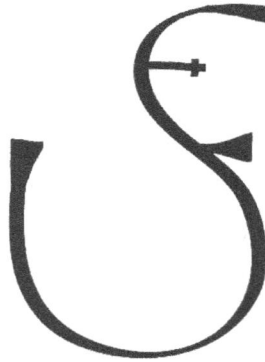

Success Sigil

Can you find the letters?

In this way you can make all sorts of sigils.

If you want to imbue it with a potion or tincture, this is the time to do it. You can either soak the paper in your tincture or brush it on. Either way you must let it dry. Overnight is best.

Now with this new image (of combined letters), inscribe it with your magical ink on your absorbent paper.

Now that you have the sigil, the next step is to breathe life into it with Pranic Breathing, also known as belly breathing. If you're familiar with yoga, you are probably familiar with Pranic Breathing techniques. Breathe in deeply; allow your stomach to inflate. Visualize pulling up energy from the earth. When you have built up enough energy in your lungs, blow it onto the sigil. This will charge it with your energy and further empower your intention.

Now place your sigil in a safe place and forget about it. Forgetting about it is the toughest part of the whole process. This helps the magick work.

As you can see, making your own sigils is quite easy and

fun. After some practice, you will be able to do them quickly and easily.

Remember the Gods are here to help. You can call on them for inner strength.

How to phrase a sentence for a sigil to get a job:

- All blocks I have put up, known and unknown, dissolve so that I am a good candidate and my future employer hires me.
- Help me express the inner strength, skills and energy so that I can acquire a job of my liking.

Here are phrases for those who have an interest in an entrepreneurial path:

- I find new ways to serve others successfully so that money comes to me naturally.
- All blocks I have put up, known and unknown, dissolve so that I can create abundance in my life.

Can you see how each sentence or phrase focuses on inner change, not the external "give me, give me"? With these phrases you are not looking for a handout. **You are creating the abundance by changing *yourself*.**

This can be applied to the rest of your magick as well. Another example is love spells. Focus your magick on *being more loving, or more open to love.* Never do love spells *upon* a particular person. Instead do a spell to attract love to you in whatever form is appropriate by creating yourself as more loving.

By focusing on inner change and developing our inner strengths, we can achieve our desires.

Goddess Has Your Back in the Worst Times

When you're reading a book what are you looking for? I'm looking for the truth and some way to become stronger. I promise to provide both for you in this chapter.

END OF EXCERPT
from *Goddess Has Your Back*
Available from Amazon.com and BarnesandNoble.com

* * * * * *

Excerpt from *Beyond the Law of Attraction to Real Magic* by Moonwater SilverClaw

Beyond the Law of Attraction to Real Magick
How You Can Remove Blocks to Prosperity, Happiness and Inner Peace

Self-perspective: Overcome the Blockage of Not Feeling Worthy

Do you feel worthy of the best that life has to offer? Maybe on the conscious level you say, "Sure. Bring it on. The new house, new car, and a real, loving relationship."

But have you ever sabotaged your chances of getting exactly what you wanted?

Self-sabotage can occur because of feeling not worthy on a subconscious level.

If it's subconscious, how can we deal with this?

Good question.

Soon I will share with you a Self-Love meditation.

But first let's talk about magick. The whole premise of this book is that there is a way to go about the Law of Attraction with more power.

To put it simply, the Law of Attraction is a form of magick, but people who read an introductory book on the Law of Attraction are often denied enough information to truly make the Law of Attraction work in their own lives.

So to really make a positive difference in your life, we need to talk about real magick. I spell magick with a "k" to distinguish it from stage magic you see on television.

Magick is a natural power, *not* a supernatural one. Who uses magick? In my spiritual path, Wicca, one is trained to use magick in appropriate ways.

When Wiccans do magick, they channel *natural* energies and create change with them.

Well, if Wicca isn't really supernatural, then why practice Wicca at all?

To put it simply, *you want something.* That's probably why you were interested in the Law of Attraction in the first place. Now in the context of learning real magick, you'll be able to fully use the Law of Attraction. And that's good news!

Everyone is different and has their own answer to that question. I like to think of religion as a bottle of wine. Let's say you have three different people who all taste the same bottle of wine. The first person points out that the flavor has accents of oak. The second praises the hints of apple in it, and the third enjoys the floral notes. They are all right. The wine contains all the flavors they described. But each person detected something different. Religion is like that. Deity can't be entirely known. So the truth of it is scattered into many faiths.

In Wicca, we honor the God and the Goddess. If that's new to you, you can substitute the label of Higher Power or

God or Deity.

The Gods and Goddesses have helped me and they can help you, too. The first thing they taught me was self-love.

Before we go further, let's make a distinction between self-love and self-conceit (or being stuck in one's ego).

Self-love is about kindness and support. So it's a good thing. It is NOT about your ego or puffing yourself up.

Let me show you how the Gods changed my perspective on myself for the better.

One of the best exercises I learned is meditation. Through reflective meditation, the Gods helped me understand how skewed my perception of myself really was. This was a key turning point for me.

One thing you always hear about are affirmations, but for many of us these just don't work.

First, let's cover what an affirmation is. It's a personal, positive statement. It can be as simple as "I feel terrific" or "I make a lot of money."

For many, the above statements don't work. Why?

A number of people have said, "It just sounds like I'm lying to myself."

Like myself, many people's inner self-beliefs interfere with these positive statements. For an example, if I used the affirmation "I am thin," my brain would object with "No, I'm not. Look in the mirror." It's not true. No matter how hard you try to pound that new idea into your brain, your brain pounds just as hard back.

So how did the Gods help me deal with this problem? They inspired me to create a Self-Love Meditation.

So instead of the uphill battle of an affirmation, we'll use the Self-Love Meditation to work with the situation.

END OF EXCERPT

from *Beyond the Law of Attraction to Real Magick*

Purchase your copy of this book (paperback or ebook) at Amazon.com or BarnesandNoble.com

Special Offer Just for Readers of this Book:
Contact Moonwater SilverClaw at askawitchnow@gmail.com for special discounts on books, consultations, workshops and presentations. Just mention your experience with this book. Thank you.